How I Found Myself

In Egypt

Subhanah Wahhaj

Acknowledgements:

I would to thank the Only one responsible for my existence. The word Muslims use for God is: "Allah" and therefore many people mistakenly use the word, "Allah" to refer to: "The Muslim God" or the "God of the Muslims" but this is a HUGE mistake. There is ONLY one God and this is the Lord of the Christians, Muslims, Jews, Hindus, Buddhists and people belonging to ALL religions and races. Praise God!!

HOW I WAS ABLE TO DO ALL THIS:

You will not truly appreciate everything your parents have done for you until you have children of your own.

I want to not only thank my Mother but recognize her. We don't give mothers their due recognition for all that they have truly done for us; Pregnancy and child labor are laborious, let alone the early years, when babies are highly dependent on their mothers for EVERYTHING! I just want to publicly thank my mother for all of the patience, hard work and compassion she employed raising me and my siblings. She raised 9 children! She is courageous and she has heart!! Thank you Mumzie for showing me that ALL things are possible!

Oh and after all that she had done for me, she enthusiastically joined my book launch team. I thought that was so awesome!! Thank you, Mumzie. I could never repay you!!

I happen to have a famous father, Imam Siraj Wahhaj but even before he was famous, he was my father. Because of his dedication and commitment, my siblings and I attended Islamic school, which was instrumental in me having the foundation that I needed. For that alone, I am ever indebted to him.

When first edition of book came out, he took books with him everywhere, selling them and even sold it internationally to more countries than I have enough room to list here. The exposure of the book increased profoundly because of him. And he also wrote the beautiful foreword for this book. Thanks so much Dad. I could never repay you!!

MY SUPPORT TEAM

Your support allows you to write without disturbing you. Your support takes initiative and helps whenever and wherever he can. Your support takes the children off your hand sometimes so that you can rest, write and take care of business. I want to thank my husband for being my biggest support! Without you, I wouldn't be able to do what I do. THANK YOU!!

Included in my support team is my mother, father, sisters, brothers, Um Jamellah, Sr. Wadiyah, my grandmother and all my beloved friends. They take a huge load off me and offer acts of kindness that I could never repay. THANK YOU!!!

THANK YOU Sister Jamilah El- Amin. I can't thank you enough for the outstanding job you have done in editing my manuscript and providing me with such an amazing updated version of my book. Not only are you very skilled at what you do but you are a joy to work with!

THANK YOU Sharon Davis, you are more than an editor, you have provided us a wonderful resource and you are an invaluable member to have on anyone's team. Thank you for your willingness to edit additional work on such short notice! And thank you for your outstanding work!

A HEARTFELT THANK YOU TO THE WRITE PATCH for the quality and excellent services you have provided for me from getting my book published to exemplary other services ranging from cover art and production, advertising and production and so much more! Allowing authors to self-publish and keep their rights while guiding them along the way is brilliant!!

You are a team of hardworking, reliable and caring individuals!! And what you have provided for me can never be matched!!

Wholesale and promotion:

Wholesale orders and discount of books in bulk contact:thewritepatch@yahoo.com with subject heading: wholesale.

For promotional copies free of charge, contact:thewritepatch@yahoo.com with subject heading: promotion.

Are you an author or prospective author looking for services or help? Contact: thewritepatch@yahoo.com with subject heading: services.

MY BOOK LAUNCH TEAM:

My mom and Dad, The Wahhaj Family, Maryam Leveille, Ameera Rahim, Zahira Rahim, Mary Booker, Michelle Miller and Kesha Hill. THANK YOU FOR ANSWERING THE CALL AND ON SUCH SHORT NOTICE!! I REALLY APPRECIATE IT!!

ALL THE PEOPLE WHO HAVE EVER SUPPORTED ME, ENCOURAGED ME, OR HELPED ME IN ANY WAY, THANK YOU!!! YOU KNOW WHO YOU ARE. THERE WERE TIMES WHEN I WAS REALLY DOWN AND SOMEONE LIFTED ME UP WITH A SMILE OR ENCOURAGING WORDS THAT KEPT ME GOING!!!

NEVER BELITTLE ANY DEED AND NEVER PASS UP ANY OPPORTUNITY TO HELP SOMEONE. YOU NEVER KNOW THE FRUITS THAT WILL GROW FROM THAT!!!

Last but DEFINITELY not least, I want to thank YOU, the reader. Thank you for reading this book.

If it wasn't for YOU, I wouldn't have anyone to exchange my ideas with. (What fun is it having a book that no one reads?) And the reason, I say exchange ideas as opposed to share ideas is because that is my aim. I do NOT want to just load you with my ideas. I would like to hear from you too and that is one of the things I would like to facilitate on my website:

http://SubhanahWahhaj.com

My website is being reconstructed as I type this now but before you know it, it will be up and running, Insha Allah (God willing). Make sure you check it out and subscribe, we've got all types of GOODIES FOR YOU!!

THANK YOU ESPECIALLY:

I want to specially thank YOU for purchasing this book. Your support allows me to continue my writing and hopefully produce work more that will be of benefit to humanity. By purchasing my books and products, you join me in making a difference, so I want to say: THANK YOU!! I COULDN'T HAVE DONE IT WITHOUT YOU!!!

As always, I thank you for posting your reviews on Amazon. These make a HUGE deal! Essentially by doing so, you will be contributing to the success of the book, to it gaining more exposure and ultimately to more discovery, which I hope will have a more positive impact on the world, so thank you so much for taking the time to post your reviews on Amazon.

Finally, thank you for your support!

Find me on facebook! Friend me and send me a message that you bought my book and I'll accept your friend request. That is the least I can do!

I look forward to connecting with you! Take care and God bless!!

Foreword

This book really blew my mind! It was so good it was delicious and it just so happens that the author happens to be my daughter, Subhanah Wahhaj. It reminds me of a book I read called "Growing up X" by Ilyasah Shabazz, the daughter of Malcolm X. The only difference is Malcolm X never got a chance to read his daughter's book and I got a chance to read my daughter's book. How I found myself in Egypt is extraordinary and riveting! I wish you get a copy today."

Imam Siraj Wahhaj

Chapter 1

In the name of Allah, the Most Beneficent, the Most Merciful

"See they not that they are tried once or twice every year (with different kinds of calamities, disease, famine, etc.)? Yet they turn not in repentance, nor do they learn a lesson." (Quran 9:126)

The eyes of students were glued to the TV, watching as the plane went crashing into the World Trade Center. I watched too but with stilled emotion, not realizing the magnitude of what had taken place. I'm sure it was an accident, I thought to myself and casually went about my day. It wasn't until it was reported that Osama Bin Laden claimed responsibility and Muslims were attacked that I came down from my innocent little cloud and realized the implications of what had taken place.

I had been on my way to a morning class at Medgar Evers College when it was announced that courses for the rest of the day were cancelled, so I decided to go the Mosque as I usually did between classes. When the crowd of people waiting for the bus steadily increased without there being any bus in sight, I knew something was wrong. I left the ever-hopeful people at the bus stop and began to walk the 15 minute hike as I did on occasion. It wasn't until I reached closer to my destination in the Bedford-Stuyvesant neighborhood that I came in contact with more pedestrians; it was a moment that changed my life forever.

I struggled to unwrap myself from my mother's warm quilt and tried ever so hard to motivate myself to get out of bed and get ready. Just the thought of what could be waiting out there for me once I stepped out of the door frightened me. With no one to accompany me to school, I had better be ready to brave what I would face.

I was dressed in a flowery, navy blue skirt that covered my ankles, a long sleeve shirt and a blue hijab on my head, pinned at the neck and draped over my chest. I could have easily blended in with the society if I wanted to, without any worry of being attacked. During that time my brown face and obvious African-American ethnicity would not have caused offence, since it was lynching season for the Muslims and Arabs, not those noticeably non-Arab. But my Islamic garb identified me as Muslim and made me a moving target. As scary as that was, I could not remove my hijab. The firm Islamic principles imbedded in me by my parents, made me stand firm even in my feebleness. I said Bismillah, offered dua and proceeded to the bus station around the corner, where my hour-and-a-half commute on public transportation from Jamaica, Queens to Brooklyn would begin. There was no turning back.

"Religion is a bunch of rituals!" said the Psychology Professor. Did I hear him right? Shock inhibited my speech. I was appalled that he would make such a bias comment. By the time I recovered, the professor had already moved on to another topic. Besides the missed opportunity, I was not in a position to challenge the professor, or anyone for that matter. Trepidation was intensified and left me feeling vulnerable like never before.

The topic of Islam would randomly come up in classes and I had to be ready. I prepared myself for the animosity, rage and hate. People would repeat misconceptions about Islam, putting the pressure on me, as the only Muslim in the class to correct them. I wasn't prepared for this at all. I had a hard time speaking up in public as it was and now I had more of a reason to be nervous. I was shaken like never before.

"I don't understand that religion!" one of my Professors said to me in a conversation we had only a couple of days after the catastrophic incident. I had regarded him as someone positive and open minded and never imagined such words coming out of his mouth. Based on what was presented in the media, he had already made an assessment about a religion practiced by over a billion people worldwide. It is calamitous how many people can do so without taking the time to open the Qur'an, a compilation of Hadiths or even attempting to study Islam. Since we were talking one-on-one, I felt comfortable speaking up. I confidently challenged him and left him with something to think about. Alhumdulillah, we were able to wrap up the discussion on a positive note.

However, it didn't go as smoothly with my Psychology Professor. He was a bitter, old man who had a long line of students who often complained about him. It was said that this white man enjoyed working at a predominately Black school, so that he could derail, discourage and dissuade as many students as he could. I soon learned that his prejudice extended into the realm of Islam, and me fitting both his disgusts, caused me to suffer extensively from the brunt of his abhorrence.

My inability to respond to his contempt encouraged him to provoke me even more. I tried to put on a valiant face but felt that any moment I was going to break from the pressure. The Psychology Professor went out of his way to make me feel discomfort; to say that he took delight in seeing me squirm was an understatement. I wished I could hide my coyness and play cool, but no matter how much I tried, I couldn't. I was disappointed in myself. Why couldn't I just go in there, stare the Professor in the face, take notes and refrain from shivering from his disdain?

I did my best to avoid conflict and kept my mouth shut, except on one occasion. It was right after 9/11 in my Psychology class, when discussion was centered on the domestic security breach. One of my peers appeared to parrot what she heard as opposed to analyzing the facts to come up with her own conclusion. To my own surprise, I spoke up. I challenged the validity of her argument.

As a journalist-in-training, I knew the importance of sources being verified. However, I understood that it's much easier to take what is presented before you than to collect and discern information objectively. Whether the information is presented by a news broadcaster or in print, I didn't forget that people behind the news are not infallible. Otherwise, there wouldn't be a constant revolving door of retractions made each year.

It was only natural that I would study journalism in college; I have always been an inquisitive person, asking 101 questions--even if it's just to myself--to make sense of things. I was no lawyer and no expert, but I knew that it may take weeks or months before evidence is discovered, analyzed and a detailed investigation in launched before a crime is solved.

Moments after the plane hit the WTC, it was being reported that Osama Bin Laden, the founder of Al-Qaeda, and his followers were cited as responsible for the crime. The people were angry, and someone had to pay. If you were dressed in a certain way that people associated as Islamic dress, you became a target--which explains why Hindus and Sikhs and many others mistaken as Muslims were also pounced on.

The student I questioned was defensive. I expected this. She responded to my disparagement with more things that she heard. "They said…," she testified as if no one could tell her anything different. I don't even know why I bothered to say anything. I felt like giving up but knew that I couldn't.

My limited spiritual development made it more of a jihad for me to get by day by day. Unfortunately before 9/11, I didn't have the regular practice of soothing my soul by reading the Qur'an and making constant thikr of Allah, so trying to pick it up now was nearly impossible. Also, since I hadn't experienced my problems actually melting away while reciting the Glorious words of Allah in the original language, and I didn't realize how much I was losing by not being able to take shelter in these life-saving rituals during these trying times.

In a nut shell, since I failed to seize the opportunity to really invest in the cultivation of my spirit like I should have, I lost out. I gave some time to these practices but not the same effort and hard work that I gave to other things. I would learn the results of neglecting the spirit to be pricier than losing all of your property and wealth; if you don't check yourself, you are in danger of becoming bankrupt.

Devoting the necessary time and attention to my courses was another struggle. I wasn't able to really focus during class or open up the books outside of class. My mind wondered to my safety and welfare and that of my family and of the Muslims in general.

I never felt so physically weak and mentally drained. The unsettling atmosphere kept me on edge. My soul felt weighed down by the murky cloud of danger. But that was just the beginning.

I felt butterflies in my stomach. Something told me to expect something from the Psychology Professor. The topic in my Psychology class was related to jealousy, the feeling that usually comes over a child when their new sibling arrives on the scene; they resent sharing toys with them and may start to act out now that someone has stolen attention from them.

I was on edge, anticipating an unruly comment from the Professor until I paused for a moment to reflect. During the entire class, the Professor actually refrained from saying anything disrespectful or crude. As a matter of fact, during the last previous classes he spared me his derision and said nothing relating to religion at all. Maybe he had finally put it to rest, I hoped inwardly. But while wrapping up the session, he made his mark by topping off all the insults ever made in class; he uttered the most outlandish, uncalled for statement that I would forever remember.

"…when your husband comes home and says I want another wife," he said haughtily, tying in the topic of jealousy to a hypothetical situation where a Muslim woman may learn about her husband's interest in practicing polygamy.

The Professor sat back in his seat and gave me one of those sadistic smiles. The class was over and I was left frozen in disbelief. The comment caused me to immediately cease packing my bag and began to turn the wheels in my head, in search of a rebuttal or a response. My mind frantically tried to come up with something but it was stumped like never before from the undermined attack.

I was lost for words and found it difficult to even report him as he was the chair of the Psychology Department. Even if I complained to the President of the school, with no proof, it would just me my word against his.

The sound of the college students instigating rung in my ears, making me feel even more disrespected. There was a synchronized melody of students saying "Oooohhh!" like the little kids did when one of their peers silenced another in a joking match. Not only was the professor calling me out, but the entire class bore witness to it.

It didn't take a Psychologist to see what he was doing: the crude comments, looking me up and down and giving me dirty looks while I entered the class, and doing or saying things to direct my attention. It was clear that he was trying to push my buttons but I wasn't going to give him any satisfaction by reacting. I continued to smile and be respectful to him as I did with all my Professors. Instead of responding to his ignorance, I chose to follow the example of Prophet Muhammad, peace and blessings be upon him, who was a walking Quran.

Chapter 2

**"O you who believe! If a Fâsiq (liar – evil person) comes
to you with any news, verify it, lest you should harm
people in ignorance, and afterwards you become
regretful for what you have done." (Qur'an 49:6)**

The misinformation being fed to the masses about Islam
was overwhelming. So many untruths were being bluntly
written about Islam and the people digested it without
questioning. This was dangerous. There were people who
thought Jihad meant holy war and only Allah knows how
many people thought that the people who committed the
horrendous act were martyrs. Some of the concepts in
Islam were either distorted or laid to rest and replaced with
lies.

I held the writers fully responsible for what their hands sent
forth, for they are professionals who should actually make a

commitment to deliver the truth, instead of just portraying to do so. In addition, I faulted the Muslims for being so passive and not taking immediate action upon being misrepresented. Now, after allowing such lies to spread for so long can we really get mad when people begin to believe them? When the propaganda is even more damaging after a catastrophic event like 9/11, we have to devote double the effort, sacrifice triple the time, and invest in quadruple as many resources to convert the losses into wins.

The fight was too great for me to think that I could do it alone. I was not equipped to challenge every student or even attempt to battle every prejudiced professor on campus. I asked about the Muslim Student Association. To me, I didn't think we had a choice in the matter. As Muslims, we have an obligation to give da'wah and the MSA was a beneficial tool to do just that; dispel the myths and misconceptions, promote and encourage dialogue between Muslims and non-Muslims on campus and open the floor for information sessions, lectures and the like. If anything, this was the time for Muslim students everywhere to make sure there was an active Muslim Student Association at their school.

The MSA at my school was vacant and I was on a mission to get it revamped. After searching for Muslims on campus, I finally found a Muslim brother who was able to give me some information. He said that the MSA had been in defunct for some time, which means when it was time for other club activities, the Muslims couldn't be found. This was embarrassing, to say the least.

I went to the Student Government Office to investigate. They showed me a huge bag full of unclaimed mail.

"It's a shame because the MSA gets more mail than any other club," I was told.

I asked what I had to do to get the club up and running again. I wasn't seeking to be leader but no one was stepping up to the plate so I assumed responsibility and did what I needed to do to get the club rolling again. Alhumdulillah, before you knew it, Allah blessed us to be successful in getting the club up and running again. I also found the last president who had been missing in action. I didn't bother questioning him about the Muslim Student Association being vacant for so long. I simply told him that I was taking over now and invited him to participate. He agreed, without showing any resistance or even bothering to explain his past inattention to the club.

We established the offices. I was the president and the former President, Abdul Salam, was the Vice President. Soon after, the positions of secretary and treasurer were filled. I rushed to establish this for the facilitation of the paperwork and for the overall function of the club without highlighting the responsibility and accountability for each officer. Later on I would learn that this was a huge mistake. Since my main concern was getting the club up and running, I overlooked the importance of the members doing their part and working as a team. This was even more significant than getting the paperwork straight, because if the foundation isn't steady, the establishment would soon crumble.

Nevertheless, the Muslim Student Association was able to make outstanding progress. After a lecture by a prominent Imam, the attendees were left with a clear understanding of what Jihad actually is. One student exclaimed how happy she was now that she learned the truth about Islam. How many people out there are still in the dark?

Chapter 3

"This is a reminder and verily, for the Muttaqun (the pious) are promised for the day of reckoning." (Qur'an 38:49)

Living in America as a single, steadfast and sheltered Muslim was the hardest thing in the world. Almost everywhere you turn, you could see couples being affectionate and hearing people talk about how great it is to be in love. With people today living their moral lives like advertising slogans such as "just do it," it's an uphill battle for anyone committed to abstain until getting married. Without faith, patience, and a support system, you just may lose it.

While some mothers were prepping their daughters for marriage, teaching them how to cook meals or take care of the house, my mom was teaching her seven daughters the importance of being independent. Don't get me wrong, she did show me how to cook a couple of meals during the later stage of my development, but she stressed how important it was for us, as the women in the relationship, to empower ourselves with an education so that we wouldn't have to depend on a man for anything.

"Make sure you get that degree under your belt before getting married," she continually advised us. We were given instructions to hold out until we got our college degree; that is, stay focused and not get married until we had the piece of paper that would, in her eyes, grant us independence and financial security. She used her experience as a testimonial, re-living the painful details every time she relayed the message to us. This is what will happen to you if you don't take heed to my advice, she said in a nutshell. Don't follow in my footsteps.

As a result, I was on guard and serious about getting my education. Should my future husband, whomever that may be, act out of order, I could go about my business, with my degree and career, without worrying about how I was going to fend for myself. Momma had to do it after 25 years of depending on her husband and putting her needs and wants on the backburner just to wind up divorced and raising nine children. She now felt she had a duty to warn every female who came in her path.

I knew mom would not be happy hearing about any marriage prospects for me before I finished College. In my mind, if anything were to progress with the brother who I agreed to court me, that wasn't going to derail me from moving forward with my studies. Even though I was still on track to get my degree and didn't necessarily have to get married right away, I knew that would not hold any weight with my mother so I braced myself, knowing what to expect.

Mom didn't realize what she was doing to us by constantly reminding us of the heartache and pain she endured consequent to her shattered marriage and her attempt to put together the pieces of her life. She would find herself bearing the weight of taking care of herself and young ones still under her care, as she struggled to attain her degree. It already took me a while to come to terms with her traumatic experiences, and being reminded of them was heartbreaking. I wanted to erase her pain with a magic marker and give her permission to move on with her life. I understood her intentions were good, but I just wished she didn't use her life as a means of overshadowing what we would go through if we didn't "protect" ourselves. The scary picture painted would give a distorted view that would stay with many of us for decades. This would affect our perception of men and marriage in general. Not only that, but it would give us a negative expectation of the treatment of our future spouses. I'm sure mom didn't realize this because we ourselves didn't realize it, until we were in relationships.

 "I think you would be a good match for him," a sister from the Masjid told me. She was trying to hook me up with her friend's son. I tried not to show my enthusiasm but the thought of being intended became more intense in my mind, though not revealed to those near and dear to me. I knew it would eventually happen but it seemed like a dream. I wasn't in a rush to get married the next day, but I did crave the companionship, being able to talk on the phone and get to know someone without the fitnah. We weren't able to have boyfriends, which I agreed with and understood the wisdom behind. I just wanted to know what it felt like to float on a cloud.

 The brother was from Georgia. His mother spoke to my father and before you knew it, he took a flight to New York for a meeting with me and my dad. It was my first sit down ever with a brother and I had goose bumps. Based on the good reputation of this brother, I was sure that he would pass my father's "tests," but boy was I in for a surprise. My father liked Abdur Rahman but there was a red flag.

As my wali, my father would have the task of screening any prospective candidates for me to make sure that they were worth my time. Naturally, the father would have his daughter's best interest at heart, hence the reason why they are the natural wali of the Muslim women, guarding them and protecting them from predators.

I was ready to be intended the next day and would have made a commitment hurriedly but my dad performed an extensive examination. He was asking all the right questions and I, being so idealistic, didn't see the importance of those questions being answered. I thought I was mature enough to decide on a mate by myself and didn't see the significance in any delays; if it wasn't for my father pushing the brakes I would have ended up in a serious car accident. Though at the time I was disappointed that Abdur Rahman would only return back to the South without us being intended, years later I would thank Allah for not allowing me to marry him. Many times the youth can be impatient and stubborn, thinking they have all the answers but needing the wisdom of their elders. And though I was 18 years old, I lacked the wisdom. That temporary moment of being mad at my father for not giving us the permission to be intended actually turned into me thanking him repeatedly for going above and beyond as my wali and saving me from making what would have been the worst mistake of my life.

I really wanted companionship and wasn't sure when I would get married; this bump in the road just made it seem less realistic but I had to be patient and stay focused. Being enrolled in College was the best solution; being busy with papers and studying left me with no idle time to sit around daydreaming about the day I would finally get married. Also, it gave me a sense of purpose and accomplishment. And it's true, I've always been a real studyaholic, finding joy in learning and analyzing ideas and concepts, which is why I needed to be in school cultivating my mind so that Insha Allah, I could be in a position where I would be able to make a difference in society.

Chapter 4

"Verily! I have made that which is on earth as an adoration for it, in order that We may test them as to which of them are best in deeds." (Qur'an 18: 7)

Though I slept at night, my soul was not at rest. How could I sleep soundly knowing that all this corruption and chaos was taking place? I felt oppressed by both my soul and environment and yearned for an escape. I wanted to go away to some peaceful Muslim land where I wouldn't be exposed to such blatant sin day in and day out and where my spirit could rejoice in the remembrance of Allah. The pollution and immoral filth throughout the land made me sick to my stomach.

I craved immersing myself in the deep studies of the Qur'an and Islamic Sciences, with the hope of developing a deeper appreciation of the deen. For the longest, something has always demanded most of my attention, school, work, life. After coming home exhausted from this dunya, my spirit craved something more. How much have I really invested in my future? How often was I able to merely block out everything and just focus on my ibada, such as performing voluntary prayers, reading the Qur'an, and engaging in thikr of Allah. Just the thought of being able to do this tickled me and awakened my spirit.

My head was swirling. There weren't enough hours in the day for the things that demanded my attention: classes, studying, papers, keeping up with the MSA, you name it; every minute had to be accounted for and I had no time for social activities. I worked hard, and even when my body rested, my mind was busy at work. But Alhumdulillah, I wouldn't have it any other way. Though I moaned from time to time, wishing for the day it would all be over, the truth is I really enjoyed college life and despite always being busy, I preferred to have a lot going on rather than nothing at all.

Alhumdulillah, the MSA was really progressing. We had da'wah tables, activities and lectures. Yes, things were looking better but we were not safe from the ever-rising issues threatening the stability of the club. There were days when other students beat us to the classroom and treated it as a social gathering. Once we informed them that the room was reserved for our club, most of them left without any problems. But from time to time, there would be those who wanted to test us; on those occasions we continued our meeting, despite them being in the room. This was a rare occurrence and as a preventive measure, I tried by best to get there early to maintain order and avoid conflict.

One day while having a meeting with the door open, one of the SGA members invited himself in and took a seat. At first the members just looked at him and listened to see what he wanted. I think most of the members saw it as an intrusion but no one expressed this. We listened as this talkative person initiated conversation about religion and world events. Alhumdulillah, we entertained him that day because as Allah would have it, after asking questions and visiting the Masjid, he embraced Islam. Look at the results of having an open-door policy and having patience. One of the main goals of the MSA was to encourage dialogue between the Muslims and non-Muslims on campus and Allah facilitated this on a single instance without us even exerting the effort. God is so Great!

The following meeting, the New Shahadah, an already loquacious and excited person was energized and talking non-stop. He was ecstatic! He couldn't believe that no matter what sins he had committed, by embracing Islam, his slate was now wiped cleaned. This is the mercy of Allah; He pardons all who sincerely enters the faith regardless of what sins they had committed, small or great.

Thank Allah for the mandatory SGA meetings because had they not been binding, I wouldn't have attended one, which would have left me in the dark about the major decisions affecting all the clubs. It was quite an eye-opener, to say the least. Witnessing some of the events taking place and seeing the way things were run, made me see the importance of staying informed and being involved, regardless if it's mandatory or not.

Alhumdulillah, after the Muslim Student Association was able to re-establish its presence on campus, we invited a second Imam from the community to do a powerful lecture centered on the misconceptions of Islam. It was a great turn-out. We were glad that a lot of people felt comfortable enough to bring their questions to the floor during the Q &A session. There were many questions ranging from the role of women in Islam to polygamy.

"Are Muslim women expected to stay home?"

"Is it true Muslim men can have four wives?!"

"Why do Muslim women have to wear all those clothes? And what about the ones who cover their faces? What's that about?"

I left the auditorium feeling elated; we created a forum where valuable information was disseminated, common misconceptions were corrected and communication between Muslims and non-Muslims were facilitated. We were able to pull off another successful event and leave an astounding impressing.

While some questions could be answered with yes or no, other questions required more explanation. Yes, the eligible Muslim man can marry up to four wives but it comes with major responsibility and anyone who isn't just will have to pay consequences! Yes, modesty is required for Muslim women as well as men, which is why you find Muslim women dressed differently than the average woman in the society. But certain things are not written in Black and White. When it comes to the role of women, we see women covering much ground both inside and outside the home. It's a given that all women staying in the home would be problematic as female doctors and teachers are essential to meet the needs of Muslim girls and women in the society.

As a general principle, Muslim women are allowed to take up any profession just as long as their values aren't compromised and they are not being neglectful of their responsibilities at home. Some women prefer to focus on the home front, while others choose to make use of their skills for the advancement of the community. It is a personal choice that each woman must make after being completely honest with themselves and what they can and can't handle. Some women ambitiously enter the work field, without taking account of their children's needs and as a result risk losing their most precious assets.

They go out there fueled with a hunger that never gets satisfied, while the children they are entrusted to cultivate are put on the back burner. Since in this society women are encouraged to be career seekers just as the men, many feel a need to compete, at all costs, without taking any necessary breaks to address any pressing issues of their children's welfare. Rarely is it impressed upon women that they bring something so special to the table; they provide something that the men would never be able to offer, bringing life into the world.

Chapter 5

"The reward of deeds depend upon actions and every person will get the reward according to what they have intended." (Hadith or Saying of the Last Messenger, Bukhari Hadith)

The members of the MSA decided on the bookstore where the books would be purchased. We discussed the type of da'wah materials to be selected and distributed at the next venue. Yah Yah would visit the store, do the footwork and compose a list of books. However, the clock was ticking and I feared that we wouldn't get them on time. Since I was so used to making decisions independently, I failed to take a moment to slow down and evaluate what was important. In the midst of trying to beat the clock, I took it upon myself to order books from a closer bookstore, without including the members on the decision making process.

I thought the other members wouldn't mind, but boy I was wrong! For nearly an entire meeting, and rightfully so, they made it plain that they weren't happy with my decision. At that point, the financial transactions to seal the deal had not been completed, but that did not cause them to soften their stance against me. Though I viewed them as attacking me, I patiently assured them that I would cancel the order. It wasn't until I looked past my bruised emotions and was willing to look at the situation objectively that I realized the seriousness of my actions.

Going on my own and deciding on something contrary to the agreement of the collective group was senseless and unfair. I could understand how this caused them to be annoyed with me and possibly lose confidence in me as their leader. It was an unjustifiably wrong action; this time they actually gave their input and I blatantly disregarded it, thinking I knew better. Even if the books we agreed on had not arrived on time in order to distribute at the event, that lost would have been better than hastily ordering other books. I promised myself to use it as a life lesson. If we don't take the time to reflect and evaluate our actions, we may fall victim to the same thing again. It may be disguised in a different situation but until we learn the lesson, we will have to repeat the course.

Abdul Salam called for an emergency meeting. I thought this quite odd because this was the first time he had done such a thing. As a matter of fact, just having him attend the regular meetings had become quite uncommon. I called Hajar and gave her the information about the meeting.

"They probably wanna talk about getting more members," she offered.

"We're having a meeting because the MSA is having some issues," explained Abdul Salam, getting straight to business. He explained how it was brought to his attention that women shouldn't be leading. Here we go again, I thought to myself. He said something like that to me before but since he failed to bring the dalil, it never went anywhere.

No doubt, Allah has put a certain order in place. In general, the men take care of the affairs outside of the house as the women focus on the internal affairs. When they come together, they are able to get so much more done because the roles are defined, thus bringing order and structure. This is why men, in general are the ones who take the leadership positions; they are the ones who are leading but this is not synonymous with domineering, as the needs of all members of the household must be taken into consideration before the final decisions are made.

Leadership doesn't necessarily translate into clout; in fact, it can be quite stressful, as men are accountable for their actions and the effect they have on the family. Women have more of an advantage; they can advise the head without having to endure the stress and pressure of actually rectifying the situation. She may even turn him in another direction without being condescending or disrespectful, as the Prophet's wife did for him. It was during Prophet Muhammad's moment of distress that Um Salamah was able to offer him advice which changed history. She was exempted from facing the trials of the leader, yet she was able to exercise influence, while providing much needed repose for the Prophet; may I dare say that this is the best of both worlds.

Anyone in their right mind wouldn't seek leadership, unless the circumstances call for it. I definitely would have been satisfied being an ordinary member of the MSA had accountability been taken.

I was well aware that in general, men are the leaders. A woman has her post and so does a man and contrary to common thought, working in the background doesn't mean less value; in fact, not being in the forefront protects her from being vulnerable, as she is able to quietly spark change and make great things happen all from her comfortable abode. If you ask me, the precious gifts that God has given women far exceed any position or rank held by any man, regardless of how noble it may appear. I was not an advocate for women being forced to stay at home, nor would I argue for the other extreme.

In my eyes, there's no reason for women to feel compelled to compete with men for leadership positions. There's a reason the Islamic Shariah specifically legislates men to be Imams and leaders of nations. But, we were talking about a club here; a small band of College Students who simply came together to make a positive difference for the students and the University as a whole. Islam is not about restrictions; it's about making sense and bringing benefit to individuals and the society as a whole. Therefore, if anyone claimed that a woman leading a club is haram, they would have to provide their support.

I told them to get back to me once they had their dalil and motioned for the dismissal of the meeting.

The meeting was over, that was until Hajar interjected.

"The issue isn't about you being a woman," Hajar said.

I was puzzled. "So what's the issue," I asked.

"It's the way you organize and construct things," she said with malice.

I was shocked and offensively hurt. If anything, I thought she would have my back, being the only other female in the group.

"A lot of bad things happened this year!" Hajar said with disgust.

Hajar diverted the attention to another issue, giving leeway for them to prove how I was unfit to be President of the MSA.

I agree I made some mistakes but should that overshadow the great strides we were able to make? We were able to revamp the club, have lectures, reunite the Muslims on campus, give da'wah and provide a platform for exchange between Muslims and non-Muslims, whereby misconceptions and stereotypes were corrected and people found comfort and ease during times of turmoil.

Abdul Salam went on and on about people wanting to lead for the wrong reasons. Is that what he thought?

"The only reason I stepped in was because the MSA wasn't doing anything," I said, without reminding them how Abdul Salam was the President before me but due to his negligence, the club was no longer in operation.

"May Allah bless you for what you did but we'll take it over from here," Abdul Salam said.

I was silent and continued to listen.

Out of everyone, Yah Yah was the most gracious. Though he didn't agree with me being President either, he was very humble in his approach.

"I don't want you to think we're attacking you," he said softly.

The manner in which he spoke to me wasn't in a blameworthy manner; he simply addressed some of my actions so that we could come to a resolution. He could have really roasted me but he didn't. Though at the time I wasn't able to distinguish between his approach and the other two members' because of my shock of what the meeting was about, years later I came to appreciate his mild mannerisms. Sometimes it's not what we say but how we say it; though it was hard accepting what was said, I really appreciated the way in which Yah Yah chose his words. I had a feeling things wouldn't be the same once I stepped down as President, but I prayed and hoped for the best.

The MSA held elections for the next year. It was spear-
headed by Abdul Salam. They started off with the treasurer,
easing their way to the "top."

"I think this sister would be a good treasurer," Abdul Salam
said, referring to Hajar who blushed crushingly. Next was
secretary. There were no nominations, just an awkward
silence. I just made it easier on them and volunteered for
the secretarial position. What other position would I fill
anyway; I knew they wouldn't welcome me as Vice
President. Besides, which one of them would want to take
on the task of secretary? So, I just went ahead and took one
for the team. Now that we had a treasurer and a secretary,
we just needed a President and a Vice President. There
were three males in the room, Abdul Salam, Yah Yah and a
brother who stopped coming long ago due to his severely
busy schedule, but dropped in from time to time.

"Vice President," Abdul Salam went on… Yah Yah."

"He's only been Muslim a couple of months and he knows
more than me!" the other brother agreed.

Yah Yah tried his best not to blush.

Then we came to the position of President. "President?"
Abdul Salam said, "me," almost in the same breath.

"So you're nominating yourself?" Yah Yah asked jokingly.
"Do you even come to meetings?"

Abdul Salam never answered and it was accepted that he,
the same one who abandoned post before, would be
president.

The rational part of me ordered myself to put aside my hurt feelings, at least until the semester was over. It was crunch time, last assignments, papers and finals. What I did or didn't do now could make the difference between me getting a B or C in some subjects. I wanted to finish off strong, but it was such a struggle. I was still trying to get over the alarm of the meeting and how it all went down.

I was very concerned about the future of the MSA; in one year we were able to make up for the negligence; we couldn't afford to move backwards. Next time we may be banned from the same privileges as other clubs and may even be denied the ability to meet and establish our presence on campus. I tried not to worry about it but the concern remained on my subconscious. If someone abandoned ship before, what will be different the next time around? Unless the person experienced a significant change, it will be the re-occurrence of the same scenario, but with different people involved. And at what expense?

Chapter 6

"Man can only get what he strives for." (Qur'an 53:39)

At the start of the new semester, I regained focus and discontinued my association with the MSA. Before meetings would even be held, I told Hajar and I resigned as secretary. When asked why, I told her I need to focus my attention on my studies. Later on Yah Yah would ask me what was wrong, but I remained brief and stuck to my story, which was the truth, but just not all of it. Besides not wanting to be in the presence of the three who lead me to resign as President, my intuition told me to take a leave of absence from the club. Something told me that I needed to allow them to run the MSA without me being in the mix.

And low and behold, only after a couple of weeks under the new leadership, Hajar complained to me about the problems they were having. She recounted an argument she had with Abdul Salam, where she became highly offended because of what he told to her and how he said it. She viewed him as disrespecting her and belittling the work that she took on, which were not included in her responsibilities as treasurer. It's so interesting that I saw that coming.

"I was gonna throw a chair at him!" she angrily spit out.

I saw that coming also. It was quite ironic; they had been in cahoots to get me out of office, thinking that would change things for the better, but they failed to consider the challenges I was faced with as President and the tireless effort I exerted in trying to keep the club moving forward. Not only that, but they were not looking at the whole picture and they lost sight of the purpose of the MSA and that we need to work as a team, not blame any one person for any mishaps that will tend to happen even with the most ideal leader. There will always be flaws but you have to go back to the main objective. Is it being met? And is there someone in that position who is qualified to handle that position? If not, you have a major issue.

I cracked a smile. "Well, I hope everything works out," I told Hajar.

"Yeah right," she muttered before walking away.

"You cannot perceive God with any of your five senses; therefore, he doesn't exist," said the Philosophy Professor. I sat there smiling. Not only did he boldly make such a contentious statement, but he swiftly continued on with his lesson, leaving no room for debate. And since he continued with his lesson so quickly, there was no window of opportunity to counter his argument or give him a logical reason why he may want to re-think what he said.

If I wasn't pre-warned about this Philosophy Professor, chances are I wouldn't have been so composed. Before taking this class, a Christian girl painted a horrific picture of this man's class. I am grateful to Allah for giving me this warning because it helped me to prepare mentally and strategize, so that I could use wisdom, instead of just responding emotionally. I enthusiastically looked forward to each and every class, well aware that we have to choose our battles wisely. I saw it as a challenge and by the grace of Allah, I was ready.

Hajar told me that people had been asking why I was no longer a part of the MSA and she doesn't know what to tell them. I repeated to her what I told her in the beginning, without giving her any additional information, which she clearly was seeking. I never shared with her or any of the other members the struggle I was facing to forgive and forget and maintain focus on my studies; I never told them how I saw it as unfair for a meeting to be called without forewarning me what it was about. Not only was I in extreme shock but I felt betrayed and disregarded. Even weeks after the incident, it was a jihad for me to recuperate emotionally, without harboring any bad feelings for the members. I continued to talk to Hajar with the same friendliness and graciousness as I did in the beginning without letting her know that I was wounded. She called me from time to time and tried to encourage me to re-join the MSA or at least participate in some meetings. I told her I would consider it.

Now that I wasn't busy dealing with club-related activities, I had a little more time to spare. I joined the school newspaper and started free-lancing for a local newspaper in Queens. Journalism was very competitive so the race was on to write as many articles and get as many internships as possible. Some students acquired internships as early as their freshman year but I wasn't that fortunate. I was determined to catch up but was running into so many roadblocks. Many places wouldn't consider you for an internship unless you had a previous one. I felt like giving up. How can I ever get an internship if almost every place made it a prerequisite to complete a previous one? Still I pushed on and was grateful for my opportunity to freelance and develop my portfolio. When I started, I wasn't particularly proud of the articles that I had written. Since I was learning the literary style of the newspaper, major edits were made. But I didn't let that stop me; I was determined to improve my writing and write in a more professional style, so I continued to practice and upgrade my writing.

"I'm sorry, I'm not allowed to shake hands with men. It's against my religion," I told the interviewer.

He hurriedly moved his hand back after having extending it to greet me. He apologized repeatedly, looking for the right words to move past his discomfort. His uneasiness made me uptight.

Surely, I shouldn't be apologizing for being true to my deen but now I felt an obligation to make up for the embarrassment the man felt and I had no idea how.

I asked myself what I was doing there; to say that I felt out of place was an understatement. Here I was at a job fair with at least a hundred people around me, but I felt all alone. I had on a business suit; dark blue pants and jacket and my hijab pinned in the front, nicely draped over my white blouse.

Why would anyone take interest in me? I have little experience, only a few articles in my portfolio, no internships under my belt and I make the male interviewers feel uncomfortable by refusing to shake hands, not to mention any other discomfort they may already possibly feel talking with a Muslim. By the way Muslims are portrayed in the media, who can really blame them?

I argued with myself on whether or not I should budge on the no shaking hands rule, just to get passed the awkwardness and give the person on the other side the chance to really get to know me without labeling me a fundamentalist. Avoiding contact with the opposite sex at all costs had become ingrained in me, so something sociably accepted as shaking hands with a man was a big deal. How can I now take up shaking hands in pursuit of employment? It's not such a big deal, I'd tell myself, while reminding myself about Allah's mercy. But would I be considered unfaithful by shaking hands with males? After all, if I'm meant to get the job or internship I'll get it, regardless, right? Isn't it better not to compromise my principles? I desperately needed advice but who could I turn to? If there were any Muslim journalists out there, I didn't know one. I could speak to an Imam, but would he really understand my dilemma? I imagined him dismissing my problem and encouraging me to remain faithful, without offering me any practical advice on how to deal with these matters in today's world. I tried not to let this trouble me too much and remained on the hunt for internships.

I was the most enthusiastic, hardworking and ambitious student in my journalism class; I gleefully went above and beyond. I was the first one in the classroom and the last one out. I sat in the front of the classroom and asked as many questions as I could. I looked forward to going out in the field, chasing leads and drafting the articles to perfection! The class was a real confidence booster and it brought me even further ahead, by Allah's permission. There was nothing like sowing and sitting back to enjoy reaping the fruits!

I finally learned why I was having such difficulty finding an internship. I was looking in the wrong places! I needed to look at the smaller establishments, weekly newspapers, not the daily ones because they required more experience.

After meeting a freshman who acquired an internship at a weekly newspaper in Queens, I jumped on it. Surely if she was able to get something with no prior experience in the field, I should definitely have a shot. I e-mailed my resume to the managing editor and sold myself in a cover letter. In a nut shell, I was showing him that he has to be crazy not to hire me.

The result: I ended up getting the internship. I was ecstatic! After the long journey, Allah hooked me up. And the best part was I didn't have to compromise my principles. The managing editor was so impressed that he hired me before even seeing me, thus eliminating the anxiety and pressure of wondering how I would handle the "hand shaking issue." He responded to me right away and told me I could start the following week. The Creator is so Magnificent!

I arrived bright and early, ready to start my new internship. I was grateful for the opportunity and amazed at the way it happened. Who would have known a conversation with a freshman would lead me to joining the newspaper? God knew and He's the best of planners!

I stepped into the weekly newspaper establishment, wishing people a good morning and smiling. It didn't take long for me to realize that I wasn't welcomed. I was the only Muslim and African American in the entire place. It was a White neighborhood so judging by the way they treated me,

I was the first Muslim and African American that they've ever come in contact with.

People stared at me and gave me disapproving looks. I attempted to build a rapport with my new co-workers but many of them avoided eye contact with me at all costs and passed by me as if I didn't exist. I grew immune to it; I wasn't hurt or disappointed. It was expected, though very sad, given the responsibility of journalists to be objective and fair. How can one be objective in their writing if they aren't disciplined enough to examine their pre-conceived notions about others and seek the truth?

I wasn't going to let their petty behavior change me. Though it was quite discouraging to have my warm greetings ignored and my cheery smiles countered with frowns and malevolence, I made the decision to remain upbeat and outgoing; it didn't matter if no one ever acknowledged me, I didn't feel right passing by the same people every day without saying anything at all.

I knew they were intimidated and fearful of what they didn't know, which is why I didn't feed into their negativity. I wanted to show them there was nothing to fear. It's true, they may not know much about Islam or who Muslims are, but they will remain ignorant until and unless they are willing to come out of their little box and broaden their horizons.

I was grateful everyone wasn't sour. The managing editor, the person who hired me, was very friendly and kind-spirited. His warmth made up for all of the acrimony I ever felt in that office. It was a blessing too because he was the one who supervised me and he was the one who would evaluate me. Could you imagine if I had to report to someone who abhorred me or treated me as if I was invisible? I would have been in big trouble. But Allah knew what I would be faced with so He was merciful enough to bless me with a respectful and courteous supervisor. Which of the favors of your Lord do you deny?

Chapter 7

"The forgiver of sin, the Acceptor of repentance, the Severe in punishment, the Bestower (of favors). None has to be worshipped but He. To Him is the final return." (Qur'an: 40:3)

I paused when the editor-in-chief of the school newspaper asked me my opinion about homosexuality. This was something that tormented my subconscious mind and caused me much toil.

I turned to the Scriptures which mentioned homosexuality. In the Qur'an, Allah gives us an account of the people who practiced sodomy. They were given chance after chance but when they insisted on committing this sin, they were hit with something so catastrophic that terribly shook them and caused them to regret acting on their whims as opposed to following the natural order set in place by the Creator. If this was the case with them who were guilty of committing homosexuality, what would be the fate of a people who not only insist on committing homosexuality but every sin imaginable, in the name of exercising free will? Fornication alone, which at one time was viewed as a big deal among Christians, is now promoted both on and off the big screen. I found myself suffocated by people in the society who nonchalantly committed sin without much contemplation or remorse; many times these same people accused religious folks of being self-righteous, without considering that their conscious petitions those people to submit to their Higher power rather than their lowly desires.

I knew the editor-in-chief of the school newspaper was testing me. She witnessed my ability to be objective, unbiased and conduct myself in a professional manner but she also knew that I was religious. She caught me off guard. I was still deciding how I would approach the topic of homosexuality while practicing journalism and wasn't quite sure if it was possible. Would I be able to show a strong opposition to this sin and still maintain a credible reputation as an objective journalist or would I have to adopt a mild attitude towards it if my profession calls for it?

Though I have a right to an opinion just as anyone else, I've learned that race, identity, and position makes a huge difference in what one person is allowed to get away with verses another. In an age where people are threatened with losing their jobs if they say anything disapproving against homosexuality, I knew I had to play my cards right.

Someone else may be able to get away with exercising their first amendment right, but I had to be careful; I knew anything I did and said would be held against me. I didn't want to jeopardize any chances of advancing my career; I wanted to at least get my foot in the door.

The editor-in-chief looked me in the eyes and waited for my response. I avoided answering the question and re-directed the conversation to the problem of rape in the prison system. I relayed to her my genuine concern of inmates being sexually assaulted by their prison counterparts, leading many of them to alter their lifestyles. Though some may feel conflicted, instead of being encouraged to seek help, it may be easier to just push it under the rug and choose to go in the other direction. After an experience like that, without therapy and support, some of them may resort to changing their sexual preference and Allah knows best the condition of each and every prisoner in this situation.

I was not up-playing my concern for inmates; I was truly bothered by anyone being taken advantage of regardless of who they were. Our past mistakes shouldn't be a means of transgressions against us being overlooked and justified. It's not right for any human being to be raped, abused or mistreated, regardless if they are prisoners or not.

The Muslim Student Association had officially been dismembered and rendered inactive again. Hajar, Abdul

Salam and Yah Yah weren't able to get it together. After having many arguments with Abdul Salam, and attempting to move forward with the club, Hajar finally gave up and the drive that Abdul Salam had at the end of my term to "stay on top of things" suddenly disappeared once I left the picture. He went back to his previous practice of not showing up for meetings. The Vice President stopped attending meetings as well and on many occasions Hajar was the only one there waiting; she walked away disgruntled, vowing not to bother with the MSA again.

"You look so beautiful!" one of the colleagues from the newspaper said to me. I couldn't believe my ears. This woman was probably the most adamant in screwing up her face at me when I attempted to propose a greeting. She went from not acknowledging my presence to complementing me on my dress. I could hardly believe it; her mannerisms changed towards me overnight. Before you knew it, she was asking me the proper name for my headdress and we had established a rapport. I would have never predicted this in a million years. I had accepted my co-workers for being who they were and in the process of being affable, this woman had a change of heart. Since then, there wasn't a day that passed without us conversing. Even when among her colleagues, she still talked to me naturally, without any hesitation or embarrassment. I respected her for doing so and commend her for doing what most people won't allow themselves to do: let go.

There were a few other pleasant and respectful people from the newspaper establishment who I conversed with from time to time. Prior to this, I hadn't had much interaction with Whites. Aside from having a Caucasian teacher once or twice, I may have come across a handful of White people here and there.

All the schools I attended were populated by Muslims, until attending public school, where there would be an exchange from Muslim students, to students who pretty much had the same skin-color but different religion.

I never shied away from being around White people. As a matter of fact, when it came to attending colleges, I considered attending a predominantly white school, but in the end was content where Allah placed me; surely, Allah is the best of planners.

Though this was one of my few times interacting with White people, it really wasn't a big deal to me. I never felt intimidated being among them nor did I feel a need to prove myself worthy of being in their presence. Some Black folks find themselves working or living among Whites, and begin thinking too much of themselves. I knew better than that. Just because I happened to work among Whites, that didn't make me any more special than I already was. The true criterion for determining superiority is our hearts, our deeds and our reverence for our Creator, not the color of our skin. In fact, even our skin color is determined by God, so how can we take credit for that? How dare we attempt to set a value on people or judge them based on their race or religion? Ranking people is Allah's job and anyone who attempts to take it on will never be qualified to do so.

I was starting to feel sick to my stomach attending the internship. I was surrounded by toxic people who would continuously curse, complain and back bite others. I wished I could wear a pair of headphones and tune out everything they had to say; I spent the day wishing that perhaps my spirit would be spared from their abuse. I could tolerate people ignoring me and making me feel unwelcome but this other behavior was killing my spirit. I sat in the back area, literally surrounded by three individuals who couldn't help their distasteful behavior. They talked about their co-workers ferociously yet met them with smiles and pleasant conversation. If this is what they did to their White counterparts, what could I expect from them?

They smiled at me, responded when I wished them a good morning and even struck up conversation with me from time to time. I was friendly but limited contact with them; I made small talk with them but stayed focused on my work. I didn't eat with them or engage in much activity with them. I understood the mentalities that I was dealing with so I had to do what I had to in order to keep myself stable. I prayed for them and looked forward to the day my internship was over.

The managing editor couldn't stop complementing me on my first completed article. I was embarrassed by how much he praised me. To me, I didn't have any other choice but to do my best. In fact, being that I didn't expect to get recognition made me more focused on the mission at hand. Therefore, whether I received praise or not, it didn't matter to me; not receiving praise would not disappoint me and receiving praise would not go to my head. The article made it into the newspaper, without hardly any edits being made, if any at all. I was developing into the craftier journalist that I dreamed of becoming. I was so grateful to my Lord!

"I want you to leave your work and come with us. We're taking you to lunch!"

I looked up from my computer. It was the managing editor. It was my last day interning and they surprised me by treating me to a restaurant in the area! My heart melted. They thought enough about me to treat me to lunch! I was so grateful for what Allah had done for me and what he was saving for me. I looked back to my days of searching endlessly for an internship and only finding roadblocks; all of that was meant to happen for a reason. God appointed the freshman to tell me about the Weekly Newspaper and secured a place for me there. Not only that, but he used me as a vessel that would open up the hearts and minds of individuals at the establishment and have a lasting impression on them. I was taken aback at the way Allah made everything happen. We can never predict the way Allah works but we can rest assured that in the end, everything will work out just fine.

The original members of the Muslim Student Association were nowhere to be found and the MSA was immobile for a full semester. I waited and watched to see if anyone would take action but nothing happened. A part of me wanted to walk away but my conscious wouldn't let me rest. I went back to the SGA and began a similar process that I did initially to get the MSA restarted. But this time instead of giving myself the responsibility of leadership, I reached out to the new batch of Muslims enrolled in the University and relayed to them the importance of the MSA being re-established; they seemed to be motivated and agreed to attend the first meeting. Alhumdulillah, though we had been defunct, our privileges for using the room, designated for the club, wasn't taken away. I wanted to be involved in the club but I realized the wisest thing was for me to take a back seat. I was on my way out of the school and needed to remain focused. I decided to provide support and advisement from a distance until things were established. It was a rocky start but Alhumdulillah, AFTER DIFFICULTY COMES EASE! The brother who rarely attended meetings due to his extremely busy schedule, not only came back to the club but he assumed responsibility as president. He did a wonderful job and never showed any negligence in the least. I couldn't have been happier.

Chapter 8

**Why should Allah punish you if you have thanked Him
and believed in Him. And Allah is All Appreciative (of
good), All knowing." (Qur'an 4:147)**

After all the pain, sweat and tears, the time for me to
graduate finally arrived! I walked across the stage and
exhaled, knowing that I would be able to benefit from the
seeds that I sowed. I didn't have a job right after graduating
but I wasn't worried; I afforded myself the time to
rejuvenate and take a breather before getting back out there
and continuing my job search. I had a job offer on the table
from the newspaper where I interned; it was mine for the
taking but I declined. The environment would have
polluted me; my insides were already suffering being
around those toxic individuals just one day a week; imagine
if I worked with them five days a week. I considered it, at
least until I got something better but I couldn't do it; I

wasn't going to oppress my spirit even further. It was one thing if I didn't have a choice, but I reminded myself that I had options. I thought, I don't care if it takes me a couple of months before I find something; it's better to be patient and find some place suitable, than to settle and regret it later on.

After sending out my resume and going on a couple of interviews, Allah blessed me to find something, but it wasn't a job that I applied for; it was a blessing that God dropped in my lap, from a different avenue; He was pulling me in another direction, little did I know it.

One of the faculty members from my College invited me to work at her non-profit organization, the Center for Black Literature. The position was Program Coordinator. Since I interned there, while in college, I had a taste of what I would be doing had I decided to take up employment there. I was honored she thought enough of me to work there. Though it wasn't in the journalism field, I sensed it would be worth my time and attention to join this reputable organization.

I was the person behind the scenes to make sure that everything ran smoothly; I dealt with the administrative side, pulling strings, helping to organize events, following up with matters and trouble shooting. I got to work early in the morning and often times returned home late. I worked on the weekends when functions were held and assisted in setting up and filling in whenever help was needed. Though I wasn't always compensated monetarily for the extra time and work, the experience was a reward in itself, not to mention the sense of accomplishment I felt after seeing how nicely everything came together. What impressed me the most were the programs put together for inner-city youth in the community. A curriculum was constructed to implement a creative writing course, thereby giving the students an outlet to express themselves and have a sense of accomplishment by showcasing their work at the end of the program. There was nothing like witnessing the work produced by the students. It made me so proud of all the teachers, artists and other individuals who came together and worked so beautifully to cultivate these youngsters and bring about such a wonderful performance at the end of the program.

On one occasion, the extraordinary revolutionary Sonia Sanchez was invited to speak to a group of students from a local high school. I attended early to set up and do my duty, not realizing the magnitude of the event. Though the program was for the students, I was left feeling empowered, invigorated and rejuvenated. Not only did Sonia Sanchez's genuine talk shape the youngsters but it affected the adults too. Moments like these made all the extra hours and time exerted worth it. It helped me to stay focused and maintain gratitude. We may not always get compensated for our work but should we stop, knowing the work has to get done?

Meeting Sonia Sanchez in person and hearing her speak was priceless. Working at the Center has allowed me to realize the value of bringing about change-provoking events like this one. It was an honor to be a part of a revolutionary change, to reach out and touch the lives of those who are often ignored and struggling to find something to live for. Stimulating minds stimulated me, and I was so grateful to take part in this most revered act! The Center for Black Literature put on conferences, functions and events where thought-provoking ideas were shared, debated and considered. People were able to hear from the less popular writers, some who may be censored or downplayed compared to those more popular. I was appreciative for the privilege I had of being exposed to some of the most brilliant and gutsy writers, most of whom I probably would never have heard of had I remained austerely committed to the mainstream literary medium.

After working at the Center for Black Literature for about a year, I was extremely grateful for reaching such an astonishing milestone and was ready to graduate to the next stage. No doubt, it was an incredible experience working there but deep down inside I yearned to do more.

The editor-in-chief of my school newspaper sent an e-mail to undisclosed recipients informing us about a job opening at a daily newspaper where she worked. It was a part-time, administrative assistant position that she held. She was hoping to find a suitable replacement as she was on her way out. I thought it would be a great opportunity for me to get back into the journalism field so I displayed interest in the position. She told me that she'd get back to me. I knew something wasn't right after a few weeks passed and I still hadn't heard from her. Instead of waiting for her to respond to my e-mail, I called her and she informed me that she spoke to her boss about me. Great! I thought to myself, until I discovered exactly what she said to her. I was shocked when I learned what she said.

"I told my boss I know someone but the only problem is she's Muslim," the former editor-in-chief said to me.

I had to take a moment to compose myself. Did I just hear my colleague right? Someone who knew me, who could vouch for my tenacity and great journalistic skills, someone who knew I was beyond qualified for the job was presenting the possibility of me working there as a problem simply because of my choice of faith. I never saw my religion as a problem but apparently in her eyes, there was an issue.

"I don't know if you'll be willing to take off your burka, what do you call it?" she continued. I was insulted. Not only is it a problem for me to be Muslim but I should be the one to give up my first amendment right and abandon my commitment to this life-long practice of covering my hair in order to be socially accepted and allowed to work someplace.

"It's a hijab and no, I'm not willing to take it off," I responded with poise.

I was able to mask my emotion while listening to her explanation. I felt disappointment and sadness well up inside of me, as the rising emergence of anger threatened to take over. I was disappointed in her action of forewarning her boss, sad that my work ethic wasn't good enough to get a job that I was suitable for and angry knowing things like this happen all the time; people are discriminated against and denied opportunity before they even have a chance to get out there and show that they are just as good as their opponent or even better! I needed to give myself time to deal with my emotions, but not now. I wrapped up the conversation with her on a good note, wishing her success in her new endeavors.

"I don't understand the significance of you telling them I was Muslim," I told her. She told me something about "knowing how they are," which I guess insinuated that she was trying to protect me. But I wondered if this was the case or if it was her reputation that she wanted to protect. I mean, who wants to be known as the person who put in a good word for a Muslim? But I gave her the benefit of the doubt. Who knows if this was really the case? She encouraged me to still apply for the position. Though I was convinced they had already made up their minds, I made the decision to do everything in my power to create favorable results. I know that we can only get what we work for. It mentions in the Qur'an in the 39th verse of Surah 53: "Man can only get what he works for." So I intended to give it my all and let them get to know the "real me" without the pre-conceived notions and labels.

I wasn't mad at my colleague; I accepted what happened and moved on. It was an eye-opener and a major learning experience. At the end of the day, if I was meant to get the job, I'd get it, regardless of what she or anyone else said. It's in Allah's hands and everything that will happen is already written; we just have to make sure we make the right decisions.

I made it my mission to be so sharp that they had no choice but to feel compelled to hire me. I went above and beyond critiquing my resume. Even when I was certain there were no mistakes, I looked over it again and got a fresh pair of eyes to examine it.

The former editor-in-chief was very helpful in aiding me through the revision process. I was grateful for her assistance and felt indebted for all the things I learned from her over the years. I didn't condemn her for what she said to her boss; only Allah knows her intentions and her heart, not me.

I was appreciative that Allah allowed me to construct a flawless resume and cover letter. I put my heart into writing the ultimate cover letter without any embellishing. After devoting hours upon hours on my resume and cover letter, I came back with fresh eyes, only to look for more ways to make improvements. I must have thrown away thousands of pieces of papers with printed resumes and cover letters. After reviewing, critiquing and editing and reaching a point of absolute satisfaction, I printed the final product on the best resume paper available and put it in a fancy resume folder and enclosed it in a matching envelope particularly meant for resumes.

The result: I didn't get the job and wasn't even called for an interview. But it was okay because I prepared myself for it. It turned out that Allah saved me from having that job, only to replace it with something better. He blessed me to take a tutoring position at my former college where I would not only get paid more but gain valuable teaching experience that would prove very fruitful. So everything worked out in my favor anyway! Also, that would be the last time I would seek a position in the journalism field, turning me in a totally different direction that I fell in love with. So I thank Allah for not decreeing that they hire me. It just confirmed how valuable it is to believe in the All Knower and not lose faith when things seem like they're not going our way.

I sat in one of the seats nearer to the podium and listened attentively to the Shaykh giving the seminar. I was taking an Islamic class on the branches of eman and I was super-enthused; this is what I lived for--to be able to devote my attention to the studies of the Qur'an and Sunnah without something else stealing my attention. I was finished with school and I left my job. Now attending Islamic classes would take precedence and I had the flexibility of including invaluable things in my schedule like spending more time reading the transcendent verses of the Qur'an and pondering on them. There was nothing like this feeling!

"Oh! There she is!" an excited voice cried out. I turned around from the vending machine and saw two sisters smiling at me.

I was surprised. "You were looking for me?" I asked, almost in a state of confusion. I had never met the two sisters prior to their approaching me.

"There's a brother interested in you!" one of the sisters responded.

"What?!"

Apparently a brother from the class took interest in me but I had no idea. He requested his friend to ask his mother to inquire about me. I could hardly believe it! I came to learn, not expecting to link up with a brother. I had no idea who the brother was or what he was about but the fact that God allowed this brother to spark interest in me at this time confirmed my faith. Allah does everything in His timing and who knows better than He?

Chapter 9

"Verily, he who fears Allah with obedience to Him and is patient, then surely, Allah makes not the reward of good doers to be lost." (Qur'an 12:90)

Everyone was seated in the Masjid, waiting for me to make my grand entrance.

My mom turned to me before walking in and asked with a bright smile: "Are you ready?" I exhaled.

As I walked in, I heard a synchronized hum of "Aww!" From their reaction, I'm guessing they were blown away by my wedding dress. I briskly walked to the front of the Masjid to meet my father, the Imam, and my husband-to-be who had been waiting for quite some time for me to arrive.

My dress was white with elaborate pink trimmings sprinkled throughout. To top it off, I wore a sparkling crown that my mother had brought for me. Yes, after 25 years, this little princess was about to form a union and embark upon womanhood.

We had courted for about a year; we'd quizzed each other about our convictions, ideas and standards and had a general sketch of our plans together as we planned for a family. We didn't agree on everything but we were okay with that; at least we were on the same page and we were willing to work with one another and compromise.

My sister tightly embraced me. "I'm gonna miss you!"

I gave my last hugs to my family and friends and we made our exit out of the Masjid. But after our driver raced us to the airport and we waited in line and got clearance through security, we were in for a major surprise. The time printed on our e-tickets was wrong! While we thought we made good timing, the departure time was actually 30 minutes before we were ready to board. What were we going to do? We had two, non-refundable, one-way tickets to Egypt.

But something unbelievable happened. By the grace and mercy of Allah, we made it onto the plane! They had made a couple of announcements for the two missing people to board the flight and although we didn't surface, something stopped the pilot from flying. It was so clear that it was none but the High Almighty delaying the flight for us. We were meant to be on that flight, and our Lord above had something in store for us!

Visiting Egypt for the first time was an incredible experience! Once arriving in Cairo, nicknamed "Little New York" for its bright lights, highly polluted areas and large tourist attraction, we didn't feel far from home. Upon arriving at our hotel we immediately prayed to our Lord and showed gratitude for the enormous blessings. How could we sufficiently thank Him for all the blessings He's poured on us from the beginning; guiding us to go to Egypt, making everything smooth for us, saving us from missing our plane. Just the blessing of allowing us to meet the way He did, allowing our families to gel so perfectly and peacefully to work together for the benefit of the two of us, and allowing us to actually get married and have a flawless wedding day, was enough to keep us in sujud for a lifetime--and that was just the beginning. What more could we ask for? I was extra appreciative that my Lord blessed me with such a great husband who was perfect for me. He was compassionate, humble and serious about his deen. His bottom line was Qur'an and Sunnah and I loved that; and what's more, he gave me encouragement and assistance when I needed it. After all that time, not knowing when or if I would find that special one, Allah was saving him for me at this appointed time. After 25 years of singlehood, the time had finally arrived. After feeling like I was getting close and then nothing, being disappointed a couple of times, and then witnessing that Allah was not teasing me, I realized that He was saving a huge blessing for me at the time I would be ready for it. Not only that, but He removed something from me and granted me a replacement 10 times better than what I was willing to accept. Even though at the time, I didn't considering my previous marriage prospects as settling, after growing and developing, it was clear that Allah was preparing me and saving me for a mate better matched for me. God is truly the Greatest! I went from attending other people's weddings and longing for the day I too would be a bride, to finally being blessed with my own beautiful wedding day and not wishing that it would have arrived a day sooner.

"The best gift you can give your husband is your virginity," my sister told me. "Imagine how special he'll feel knowing that he's the only one you've been intimate with." These words stayed with me and helped strengthen me during the times that I wasn't sure if I would actually meet my special life partner. I was so grateful that Allah protected me from the worries of sexually transmitted diseases and premature pregnancies, and that I was able to focus on myself instead of being distracted having boyfriends and indulging in "fairy tale love." Abstinence wasn't easy but it gave the marriage something extra to be appreciated and anticipated. To me, preserving your chastity for your life-long partner, someone who was willing to commit to you and respect you, had way more perks than the "freedom" of going from one person to the next until you get tired and feel the need to settle down.

I accompanied my husband from time to time when he went to the Masjid for salah. The feeling of praying fajr, in the Masjid was like no other; I felt invigorated, energized and ready to start my day.

There was nothing like being able to spend as long as I wanted in prayer without feeling the pressure of getting up and getting back to work, school, get a paper done or take care of some other matter that demanded my time. I felt myself developing an intimacy with The Creator as I recited the glorious words of the Qur'an slowly in prayer, taking care to pronounce slowly while contemplating on the meanings. How could I adequately thank Allah for all the blessings that he showered on me: for blessing me to get married and travel to Egypt, two things had I only dreamed about! Going to a Muslim country alone was something that I've wanted to do for so long, and now doing so with my new husband was an amazing gift. After exerting the patience, the discipline, focus, forbidding myself from blindly following others and choosing to remain faithful, look at the results; when I least suspected it, the opportunity to travel and the mate with whom I would be traveling with was waiting for me.

After making salah, I remained on the prayer rug recounting all the blessings visible to me, which I realized was only a fraction of all the blessings my Lord had poured over me. I thanked Allah repeatedly. Being able to realize my dream was one part, but I was also grateful for my good health, being sheltered and protected, nourished with food, and given great parents who did the best they could with what they had. But out of all of that, I think the things most deserving of my faith was growing up with a faith that has been known to move mountains.

After staying in Cairo for about a week, we took a train to Alexandria where we would stay on campus. Allah blessed my husband Muhammad to find an excellent school where he would become certified to teach English as a second language. Soon the honeymoon period was over and my husband was feeling the pressure; after he finished the program he had to secure a job, housing, and manage our affairs in a foreign country. Islam mandates men as the maintainers and protectors of women; so while I have the choice of working or not, the strain of protecting and leading the family rests on his shoulders. Before God, he will be questioned about what he did or didn't do to keep the family afloat, and God forbid if anyone drowned while under his watch. What pressure was it to be the leader of the family! Especially for him, being that we were so far away from family and loved ones who would not want to hear about anything that happened.

Muhammad was finishing up the ESL program, and the time was approaching for us to find a new place. After talking to someone from the States who used to live in Egypt, we understood that travelers could be taken advantage of if you're not careful. We were in a difficult position because we didn't know anyone in Egypt personally; we had a few contacts, "friends of a friend," but no one we had ever met in person. One of our contacts from the States told us to let him know what area we were we preferred to rent a place and he would contact the people he knows and try to assist us to the best of his ability. But this was a stand still because we couldn't even give him an area that we were interested in. Where did we want to live? Cairo? Alexandria? We had no clue. It will all depend on where my husband found work and that was a challenge in itself. We learned that his "limitations" in his educational background and lack of teaching experience counted against him. Teaching English was quite competitive over here and he needed to stand out. He was lagging behind in the race and in a scuttle to get acclimated with the society and get ourselves established, something needed to be done.

I jazzed up Muhammad's resume, helped him compose dynamite cover letters, researched job opportunities and sent out CV's. At almost every turn, I was on that laptop. In the process of searching, I found plenty of positions that I was qualified for; I fulfilled the educational requirements and I had the teaching experience but I wasn't sure if I really wanted to work. I was still enjoying being liberated from work, school and other responsibilities that stole my time. Now I was a newlywed and I wanted to enjoy it for a minute. Also, I was hyped about embarking on my religious studies; this is what I was waiting my entire life for and finally it was here. Did I want to make a commitment to a 9 to 5 that could possibly distract me or convert my experience from a joyful one into a daunting one? Also, would I be able to work and upkeep the house and other new responsibilities that came with being a wife, while optimistically keeping up with my studies, without feeling burdened and drained? I was still adjusting to my new role as wife and that seemed to be enough on my plate, did I want to add something else that would require more discipline on my part? On the other hand, maybe this would be a help to me? I definitely knew it would help my husband and help us financially, and the blessings that come from that could be never ending. Could this be an opportunity to go outside of myself and reach a higher level? I was unsure. I asked Allah to show me the way.

My husband and I needed to find a place and no job opportunities were coming through yet. My picking up a job seemed more and more like an option. I continued to send my husband's resume out and pay attention to any signs Allah may be giving me.

Muhammad met someone who knew of an apartment we could rent. Then someone else knew about another place, and then another. Allah kept putting people in his path with better deals than the previous ones. The first place we knew about would be more than 1,000 Egyptian Pounds a month, the next one cheaper, and the next one even cheaper; we ended up moving into a place which cost us only 300 Pounds a month to rent. Allahu Akbar!

Within a week after getting acclimated into our new home, Muhammad met some really helpful brothers who extended themselves to him. Many of them invited us to their homes, and I got a chance to meet their wives. It was truly a blessing and a comfort to have people welcome us so genuinely.

We were grateful for a home, but my husband was still trying to secure employment. We had some savings but didn't want to touch it unless we absolutely had to; and even so, we couldn't live on that forever. Muhammad continued to search and I continued to send his resume out as well. I could tell he was getting discouraged. "Don't worry, Allah's got us," I reassured him. I knew he believed that but we all need a reminder at times. We talked about the possibility of me working and I told him I would make Salatul Istakharah. I forgot about the urgency of us being financially secure, and was not swayed by any outside influence. I prayed to Allah and sat in a quiet place. Allah is Ar-Razzaq, I assured myself and even if I don't go out there and work, I know He'll provide for us. The question was, is this something I really wanted to do right now. Would it aid me in getting closer to my Lord and fulfilling my mission or would it derail me from it? I sat and listened.

"No, I'm not gonna do it," I told my husband. He looked a little disappointed but I had to stick to my guns. If I ask Allah for the answer, I have to go with it; He knows and we know not.

Working outside of the home may have seemed to be the easy way out but I knew what would happen if I chose to work at that time. Allah was giving me a clear sign that working now wasn't best, and I wasn't going to pretend that I knew better.

Muhammad was looking sharp! He had on his nice dress shirt and dress pants, his kufi, and he was ready to go. He left the house early in the morning looking for work and came back in the evening with nothing, only to go back to the drawing board and start fresh again. One day he accompanied some brothers from the neighborhood to check out some schools.

"There are schools right in the neighborhood," the brothers told him.

So Muhammad planned a trip to the schools early in a morning. By this time, I started to feel bad for him, facing rejection after rejection and becoming a little less hopeful. I started to see these trips as a useless, waste of time. What were the odds that he was going to find something? But regardless, I only expressed positivity. I hid my pessimism, kissed him before he left the house and offered some encouraging words. Deep down inside, I knew Allah would take care of it; I wasn't sure when but I was confident it would eventually happen.

It never occurred to me that it would happen so soon! My husband came home smiling from ear to ear. "What happened?"

One of the Middle Schools he visited hired him on the spot. It turns out they were in need of an English teacher and since Muhammad was American, they were overzealous about having him join their team. Allahu Akbar! It was all worth it; the hard work, diligence, and me holding out. It was nothing like letting him have the satisfaction of going out there and do his duty as a man; finding the rizq that was written for him so that he could support his family. I could have gone out there and worked until he found something but I knew what that would have meant; not having me bring in any income pushed him to do what he had to do to make it happen. There was nothing like witnessing that wonder up front and center! It reassured us that it had nothing to do with luck at all; this was no coincidence, Allah wrote that Muhammad would be teaching there and nobody or nothing could have stopped it. His educational background didn't matter and his lack of teaching experience didn't count. The criteria for selecting teachers and the usual screening process did not prevent him from getting something that The Almighty had for him. I was ecstatic and so grateful to witness such a miracle. How could he have known that this school was looking for a teacher, which happened to be within walking distance from our new home, which we would have never gotten, if it hadn't been for the Grace of God. Which of the favors of your Lord do you deny?!

I walked out of the house covering my face for the first time. I had wanted to try wearing the niqab in the States but was never courageous enough to try it. I knew I had better be prepared for the stares, comments and the hostility, and I didn't want to bring on extra adversaries if I could help it. Now being in an Islamic environment eliminated all of my worries. I could try wearing the niqab in peace and determine if I wanted to take on this practice without being swayed by feelings of discomfort. It felt good, being able to wear it and not get treated any differently from those around me. I walked through the streets happily greeting everyone with "As-salamu-alaikum" and getting a cheery response. I covered my entire face except my eyes, and it was quite an adjustment. I had to keep telling myself that I could breathe fine, which was really the truth; it was just a mental thing, since my nose was covered and I wasn't used to it. Anytime we embark on a new endeavor we can expect there to be some discomfort, but I didn't truly comprehend this at the time so after wearing it a couple of times I took it off. I wasn't really sure if I wanted to wear it anyway and any inclination that this would make life harder for me was not motivation to make an upgrade, even if it was something that would enable me to earn more rewards with my Lord and possibly a higher status if done with sincere intentions.

Once I took the niqab off, I started getting more attention from those whom I became immune from while covering my face. In one instance, while in a computer lab at my husband's school, I uncomfortably found myself almost the "center" of attention, where it seemed as if every five minutes a man would strike up a conversation with me, really as just an excuse to stare at my face. Either they were captivated by my beauty or the capability of being able to see my face astonished them. Then I understood the fitnah that came along with the natural beauty of a woman. My head was covered and clothing modest, yet I was able to get such a response; imagine what the case would have been if were more revealed. This is why a woman can go out in the streets dressed a certain way and stop traffic, whereas a man can be half-naked and not even get a fraction of the response that a woman may get. While a woman has a choice to wear what she pleases, no one can deny that the natural parts of her that comprise her beauty are called her adornments for a reason.

I know that man's attraction to women can make him weak, which is why it makes sense for me to use a means of prevention to protect myself. Though men should be able to control themselves, even if presented with a woman, the reality is that there are sick men out there who either cannot or choose not to control themselves, which would be equivalent to putting a juicy piece of steak in front of a starving dog and expecting them not to bite. If you don't realize that the dog is hungry, you may use caution or at least wisdom.

This is where the Qur'an comes in. The Qur'an is the last revelation sent from God to mankind; it is a means of communication whereby the Creator is warning us and advising us. Any commandments or prohibitions given to us are only for our own good; if we choose to disobey, we will have to bear the consequences. Many of the prohibitions in the Qur'an are similar to those instructed in the Bible, as it has the same author--God.

Growing up in Islam and covering my hair was a piece of cake and became second nature. I knew that if I didn't do it then I'd be sinning and I'd have to answer to Allah for it. On the other hand, if I did do it, then every time I wore it, I would receive a reward from Allah. I was tested and if I passed the test and remained steadfast, Insha Allah, I could look forward to entering Paradise where I could do whatever I wanted and would not have to cover my hair or have any restrictions on what I wore. Wearing a hijab is obligatory at minimum but anyone who wanted to take it a step further and wear a niqab as well, could earn extra blessings and rewards from Allah.

Not long after the incident in the computer lab, I decided to wear the niqab full-time whenever I was in public. It was hard to adjust to at first but I reminded myself why I was doing it and before you knew it, it became second nature like wearing the hijab was. Covering was only a means of protection in the outside world full of predators and sick men but when I got home, I took off my hijab and niqab and was able to remove my clothes and beautify myself for my husband. After all, he is the one who I feel comfortable showing my adornments to, not some strange men.

Egyptian women were unique to me, seeming to have a perfect grasp on creating a happy and productive domestic life. They were able to host me without taking any attention away from their husbands, always checking in on them and asking them if everything okay. There was a constant revolving motion of dishes on the table; they set an elaborate display of fancy dishes on the table, fixed the plate for them, removed the dishes when they finished eating and replaced them with seconds and thirds on demand. They came back with tea, smoothies, sweets, you name it! I was in awe. I never saw anything like this! Where I come from, the women may make their husbands' plate and they may even get them something from the fridge upon request, but they don't make a hobby out of sitting there before you smiling, asking if there is anything they can do to make your dining experience even more enjoyable; she cooked it, so you better be satisfied, otherwise, you have feet, and you can use them to get whatever else you want! Watching how the Egyptian women did things made me appreciate their loving and generous spirit, but I must admit that I felt like somewhat inferior in their presence.

I felt deficient comparing myself to them. I resented doing any chores or any other "duty" if I thought it took too much of my time and I didn't really like serving my husband. A part of me felt like, at that moment, I was more like his servant than his partner. Why should I go out of my way to constantly bring him stuff from the kitchen, when he can just do it himself? I didn't get it! Why did these women do all that? Is this how a real Muslim woman should be? Was my "lack" of service to my husband a reflection of my "lack" of faith? I didn't know. I tended to get an attitude, whereas my Egyptian sisters had the pleasant disposition where they made it their duty to please their husband, family and guests.

The interesting thing is, when it came down to someone else; my mother, sister or friend, I had no problem fulfilling requests for them with a smile but when it came to my husband, something was preventing me from fully embracing him. I didn't like feeling like a maid and I didn't like feeling like I had to plan my day around him and his wishes. I didn't like the feeling of him interrupting me from my agenda, no matter how beneficial the task may be, even though I benefitted from it. It wasn't long until I realized what was happening to me. I was replaying the damaging, subconscious thought: "I don't want to relive the life of my mother."

My husband liked things to be in order and understandably so, but sometimes I would let the work pile up, making it harder on him and me. It was hard for him to function in dysfunction but to me, there was only a few things out of place so I didn't see it as a big deal. However, by procrastinating, I made the job bigger than it was, rather than just cleaning a little at a time. Unknowingly, I rolled my eyes when he reminded me of how important it was to be organized and keep things in order. Why doesn't he get off my back, I thought to myself, I'm going to get to it, not understanding the magnificence of my actions and what I was doing. All I knew was I was giving my all trying to discipline my nafs and be obedient to my husband for the pleasure of Allah, but it was hard!

Even when there weren't a lot of chores to do, I still resented it. Why do I have to do this maid work? I never said it to my husband but that's what I felt. It was boring and monotonous! I didn't like the idea of me "having" to do anything. I wanted to do what I pleased, when I pleased. Wait a minute! I knew I had to be fair. What if Muhammad had the same attitude as me when it came to working? What if he had an attitude about working and "having" to maintain me? What if he just refused to go to work, except only when he felt like it? I didn't have to worry about going out there and providing for the family. I had the option of staying home or working and if I decided to work, I didn't have to worry about paying the bills unless I wanted to help out, and I would be rewarded for doing so. Sometimes we all have to do things that we may not be particularly happy about. Our nafs wants to have paradise on earth but we have to struggle until Insha'Allah, Allah permits us to paradise and then for eternity; In Paradise there's no worrying about disciplining our nafs, just indulging in pleasures! But until then, we have to be careful because trying to indulge now without adhering to God's boundaries comes with consequences. The Creator knows what's best for us, and we weren't designed to wantonly fulfill our base desires, but to live lives with discipline in obeying God and to benefit society at large by acting morally and responsibly. Still, even knowing this didn't make struggling against my nafs any more enjoyable.

I didn't like cleaning, I wasn't a fan of cooking and I hated washing clothes mainly because it required so much effort and energy; we didn't have an automatic washing machine which made washing a multi-step process: pre-washing to get stains out, putting it in the manual washing machine, lifting the washing machine and letting it down to release the clothes, rinsing it, ringing out the excess water and then hanging them out on the line to dry. It was exhausting! And the whole way through I had to motivate myself to keep going. When it was over I needed to recuperate only to motivate myself to complete another task. Why am I here? Like many people, I like being married but I don't like the work that comes with it. But I knew it was going to take work if I truly want a long lasting, successful marriage. I could either go back to the single life where I could do as I pleased or fully embark on this journey of cooperation and respect, where I discipline my nafs and give just as I expected to take. The choice was mine.

The problem would remain there and my condition would worsen. I already had an attitude with my husband and I had some deep issues to deal with in terms of my perception and expectation of men, and what I learned about marriage from my mother and father at an early age. With something just as simple as house chores, it took twice the work because of the mental barriers that I had to wrestle with, and the resistance to be "happy Suzy maker." I didn't like myself too much with this disposition. I wanted to radiate warmth in the home, not wretchedness but in a sense I didn't know how. "You get more bees with honey," I remember my mother always saying. I wished I could be sweeter but until the bitterness at the core was dealt with, I couldn't be so sweet to my husband all the time. I had limits and still hadn't knocked down all the walls.

Why should I be the one to shut my mouth, when I know I'm right? I thought to myself. My husband and I were having another argument. While he was calm and talked with a mild tone, I raised my voice and cut him off repeatedly. He looked perturbed; I could tell he was really trying to compose himself. He finally ended the "conversation" and let me get the last word. I felt bad. Why wasn't I able to do that, just smile and let him get the last word? Somewhere in my subconscious mind I was telling myself that if I did that, I would be allowing him to overpower me and thus be submissive, something I vowed never to do. "But was that really the case," I asked myself. All I knew was, my actions weren't getting me anywhere. Most times, at the end of the day when it was time to go to bed, I felt him being angry with me without even saying anything. He would sleep with his back turned towards me. That hurt! But was it enough to spark me to make a change? I was still troubled by my convictions on what to expect from your husband after being committed and vulnerable. I wanted to trash them but how could I without replacing it with something better, and something better that I truly believed in? I read about the companions of the Prophet Muhammad (peace and blessings be upon him) and how respectful the wives were with their husbands but they were practically perfect. Could I ever be on the same level as them and have the same poise as them? My idealistic view of marriage had not only been altered but shattered. How can I ever get that back? And since the relationship between me and my husband has been battered, was there any hope for things turning around?

I was happy Muhammad spent most of the day out of the house and when he came home neither of us were excited to see each other. We barely talked to each other, it seemed, without arguing. I thought he was being too critical of me; he always had these suggestions of what I should do. It seemed as if he was disappointed that I hadn't yet picked up on my "wife intuition" and evolved beyond being self-centered. It was true. While at the time I didn't see it, he was absolutely right. When he got home, my habits would barely change. If I was on the computer, I stayed there for long amounts of time without asking when he would be ready for dinner or even taking myself out of my world to think about him for a couple of minutes. Since I was so focused on maintaining my "power," I didn't realize that it had nothing to do with being subservient; it was simply about being kind and thinking about someone else, someone who happened to be one of the most valuable people in my life. But my mind revisited the Egyptian women who so happily served those around them without even thinking about it. This is what he wants to change me into, I thought to myself, and the walls shot up. Should I constantly revolve my day around him doing things that he wants done? That's the most boring thing in the world! I didn't want to do that. Is this a level that I should aspire to reach as a Muslim woman, where I am content by simply staying in the home all day and revolving my life around my husband? I mean, I stay in the home by default, because I choose not to work at this time, but am I really happy playing this role? If not, what was the root issue that caused such displeasure? And how do I find the cure? Something had to happen because neither of us was happy.

"What's wrong?" I asked my husband.

"I don't wanna go back to that place!" he said in a melancholy tone as if he was being dragged to his death. He sat at the kitchen table with a dismal look on his face. I felt so bad for him. I knew there were issues at his job but I didn't realize the effects this was having on him. It didn't seem like a good fit at all and he was seriously contemplating leaving but the responsibility of taking care of the family must always be considered for the breadwinner.

At that moment I realized how much stress he was feeling from his job. For the first time I would care to inquire about his feelings and attempt to soothe him, as opposed to responding to his ill-fit mood by being defensive, as a result of feeling guilty for causing a damper in his mood. As a result, I had responded to his despondency with dissent rather than love. This incident was a turning point; it caused me to be more cognizant of my attitude towards him and motivated me to be less defensive and more kind to him. He really deserved it. He was a fantastic husband; he always showed concern for me and my feelings even though I didn't always deserve it and he was there for me in every way that he could. It was time for me to exert some real effort in treating him better. He was worth it. After all, this is the only person I deemed worthy enough to make a commitment to, my first and hopefully my last, if I could just get it together.

Usually after jumping rope, I was more revved up to take care of chores and do the cooking. I challenged myself to fulfill a time limit before being satisfied and putting down the rope. Starting these tasks after attaining a sense of accomplishment and joy was wondrous! It was like giving myself a pep talk. I'm doing this to please Allah, I reminded myself. I know you'd rather be doing ibada but this is ibada, and I can't think that by sitting around praying and reading the Qur'an to the neglect my other responsibilities is pleasing to Allah. It's not the most enjoyable thing to do but my account is being filled with blessings and my husband and I will both benefit. Alhumdulillah.

Out of all the people I ever met, no one made an impression on me like Um Osama; that is the mother of Osama, not the person who gained famed on September 11 but the mother of a common Egyptian brother who happened to be friends with my husband. There was no relationship to my husband's friend, Osama and the Saudi Osama Bin Laden. In fact, Osama didn't even know him, in case you're wondering. Muhammad met him soon after we moved to our new place; he lived with his parents right across from us.

Um Osama welcomed us our first night there, sending us some delicious Egyptian dishes. Not having our stove working yet, we really appreciated the hospitality. It was no accident that I met Um Osama. I got to know her personally as she hosted me in her home, taught me how to cook some Egyptian dishes and shared jewels in the form of life experience and wisdom with me upon request.

I never met anyone like Um Osama. She was the epitome of sincerity, generosity, humility and strength. She didn't have one negative bone in her body and she always said things in the best way, devoid of any criticism, judgment or abhorrence. She stood out from all the Egyptian women I met because she had a strong identity outside of a mother and wife; she was able to be who she was without any qualms and everyone loved being around her; we appreciated her genuineness; she wasn't fulfilling some duty because it was prescribed on her by her culture, having such an amazing virtuous character was a part of her. She worked outside of the home and that did not prevent her from being as hospitable and devotional as the rest of the Egyptian women; in fact, she topped all of them, being more cheerful, hardworking and patient than all of them put together. She lived to serve Allah in the best way she could, exemplifying the highest standard of character

I've ever seen. Um Osama was my shero; she was the living role model that I needed to examine in person.

I didn't feel inferior while in her presence at all, probably because I didn't have a distant relationship with her. Upon coming to Egypt and learning about the way the women tended to their husbands and families was intimidating, but the more evolved I became and the more I reflected and gradually improved my service to my husband, the less intimidated I was. Knowing Um Osama up close and personal put me more at ease and helped me not to be envious of Egyptian women for having the "training" that I never got. I still thought I was at a great disadvantage because of my background, my parents' divorce and the consequent not so positive advice from my mother, but I was beginning to chip at the wall which had been built for so long and I was making progress day by day.

I wasn't able to go back in time and change the past but I was able to put the work in now for a brighter future. I had some serious constructive therapy to do on myself but it was worth it; I was motivated to demolish the destructive habits and build a sturdy foundation, whereby I would attain peace within myself, in my marriage and do my part to raise healthy, spiritually-fortified children who hopefully won't have to go through the same thing that I did. Having Um Osama as a mother figure, someone who imparted astuteness on me and showed me so much by example was a major gift from Allah that I will always treasure!

Um Osama will go down in history as being my only friend over the age of 50. This huge age gap did not make me embarrassed or compel me to downgrade her friendship at all. It didn't make any difference to me, as a matter of fact it was a plus having someone in my circle with such great experience and insight. I felt honored to be in her presence and to witness how she was able to get it all done so gracefully: husband, children, grandchildren, career, keeping ties with her family members, being involved in the community--the true definition of balance! I admired her for that and for the work she did. In addition, she worked in such a healthy and gratifying profession; she had the best job in the world! She was able to affect change, motivate, inspire, and make a positive impact on individuals every single day that she went to work. What did she do for a living? She was a Qur'an teacher.

I happily stepped out of our apartment on my way to the school. A friend from Muhammad's job told him about the four-year Islamic studies program there and he enrolled both of us. I went from home and he went from his job on Fridays. We attended on Fridays and Saturdays and it was the most fantastic thing in the world, outside of reciting the Qur'an. It reminded me of the days I took classes with Al-Maghrib, an institute that taught complete intensive classes over the course of two full weekends. Now I could take a course for an entire semester and study more in depth. That's what I'm talking about! I was ready to sink my teeth in. This is what I wanted and now I had it. God is Magnificent!

Chapter 10

"It may be that you dislike something while it is good for you; and it may be that you love something while it is bad for you. And Allah knows while you do not know." (Qur'an 2:216)

"You're gonna have the baby there or in the States?" my brother asked me over the phone.

I didn't have a clue. "Allah knows best," I told him.

We had already been in Egypt a little over a year and just the idea of going back to the U.S. and seeing my family made me jubilant, and the thought of them being there for the birth of the baby was delightful! Feeling the way that I was, I knew that if I left Egypt, most likely I wouldn't be back. My excitement about living there was steadily declining and I was starting to wonder if I really wanted to spend the rest of my life there. My husband tried to get me to recall the good things I liked about the country. I wasn't disregarding my blessings. There were a lot of good things about the place but I wasn't sure if it was emotions from the pregnancy or if I was at the point of re-considering my needs and what's important to me. No doubt about it, my husband didn't want to go anywhere but even he was having feelings of homesickness; it came up when we were discussing my condition. I wasn't sure if I was homesick but I was starting to feel sick and tired, I don't know if it was of my environment or just life in general. I felt trapped in a boring routine, and when I looked around there wasn't much to get me excited. I woke up, cooked, cleaned, and went to bed, only to wake up the next day and do it all again. Not all days were the same, some days I managed to get some studying in, and from time to time my husband and I went out visiting friends or something of that nature; those days were the highlights for me. I felt like a wave, being pushed by the current of wind called life, just merely existing.

"You gotta get out," Muhammad told me.

"Where?" I asked.

He recommended I go take a trip to the sea, near his old school. It was a fabulous idea. It was a tourist site; they had benches where you could see the sea below and it was a beautiful, captivating view. I took the public mashoor and made spontaneous trips over there. It was a great feeling just walking the board walk and letting myself go in the breeze. Other times I would visit his old school to watch educational videos on Islamic topics and use the internet. I refrained from telling my family about my struggle; they were already concerned about the baby being on the way, the last thing I wanted to do was give them more to worry about. I would be fine eventually; I just had to ride the waves during this brief time of turmoil. I wasn't exactly sure what was going on with me but all I knew was I was pregnant for the first time and the hormones were kicking my butt.

We were getting pressure from my family to come to the U.S.; the thought of having a baby in a foreign land did not sit well with most of them, especially my mother. Every time I turned around she was e-mailing me or sending me messages, trying to convince me how it'll be more beneficial to deliver in the U.S.

"How many months are you?" my stepmother asked me on the other end of the line.

"I just gave birth."

"What!!!"

All I remember is the nurse telling me to breathe a couple of times and the next thing I knew, I woke up with my husband on the edge of my bed and Um Osama and Um

Muhammad, the mother of Muhammad's friend who happened to live a couple of blocks from me and who I developed a great rapport with, sitting a couple of feet away from me. Giving birth for the first time was so easy and smooth. How amazing is God's Favor!

I had this little life that was charged under my care. I was now a mother! She would look to me to feed her, nourish her, love her and guide her. Would I raise her to be an Egyptian who loved to serve her husband and devote herself in her home solely, raising the kids and taking care of the home or would I teach her to be independent, ambitious and career-driven? Should I direct her to be content staying in the home, instead of encouraging her to go out there and empower herself with an education like mom did with us? And if I did, what would that do for her if she is raised here in Egypt? If she is influenced by the culture to do otherwise, would she find herself resenting the culture or resenting me and what I taught her? I was so confused. I didn't really know what I wanted for my daughter because I didn't really know what I wanted for myself. I found myself being frustrated for being a square and not being able to fit into a circle. But what if I didn't want to be a circle but felt like I had to? One thing for sure, I didn't want my daughter to have to go through this! I wanted her to be at peace and feel comfortable being herself regardless.

Since there were no complications during the pregnancy and I was perfectly fine I could go home the same day. A part of me wished I could stay in the hospital a couple of days; the thought of going back home and having to get back to "work" wasn't appealing. I just wished I could enjoy spending quality time with my new baby without being tied down to a billion and one responsibilities. I was already having a hard time keeping up with everything before I gave birth, now factor in feeding a baby every two hours, changing her diapers, cleaning her, giving her comfort when she cries and dropping everything to respond to her urgent needs right away. When would I have time to bond with my baby and enjoy motherhood?

Well, Alhumdulillah, my dua was answered without me even having to make it. The day I came home from the hospital, Um Osama gave us a large container of chicken soup; that lasted a couple of days. Um Muhammad, the other sister who was there for me during my birth took it upon herself to bring over some more food which lasted nearly half a week. It was such a blessing to have good sisters in my path who sincerely cared for me and did everything they could to help me.

Not only that, but something spectacular happened. When I came home from the hospital my husband alleviated me from doing all the cooking and cleaning and happily granted me the privilege of enjoying my new baby. For four and a half weeks I was able to bond with her, take my time feeding her without being bombarded with a list of things to take care of, go to sleep and wake feeling rested for Fajr and then go back for more sleep without it being interrupted by the dreaded alarm clock. God is so Great!

Muhammad came to the bedroom with my meals, drinks and anything else I needed. He frequently asked me if I desired anything and didn't delay in carrying out the requests. His stupendous service melted my heart! Though I had given him an attitude through at least half the marriage and I barely served him with half of the care he did, this didn't prevent him from outdoing himself in trying to please me. When he entered the room, his face lit up as if he really did adore serving me. He prepared my favorite dishes, asked me if I wanted seconds and cared enough to switch things up to give me variety, knowing that after a while I get tired of having the same thing over and over again. If I have to do it, I'll endure it without complaining but it wasn't my favorite thing. He put me to shame. I felt incredibly guilty. I don't deserve all this, I thought to myself. Even after what I put him through, he consistently treated me graciously, truly reflecting his upright character. I thought back to the Egyptian women who went above and beyond for their husbands. I had qualms about them having this type of high performance when serving their husbands, but why didn't I have a problem with my husband doing so? It's all about interpretation; if a woman does it, I saw her as being oppressed, but the last word I would use to describe Muhammad would be oppressed. He chose to go above and beyond to treat his wife kindly, just like the Egyptian women did. No one was forcing them to do that; it was encouraged in their culture but that's understandable because traditionally they don't work outside the home. The way they see it, the man goes out and provides and the woman takes care of the home, so many of them pride themselves in being their best at their job. Though I don't think there's anything wrong with that, somehow in my mind I had been equating women being dutiful with being subservient. I re-visited what I saw take place between my parents and then understood why. Now that I recognized what happened to me psychologically, and my husband showed me there's no reason for me to resent serving him and in fact he was willing to serve me with no problem, I was faced with the daunting task of finding the courage to release myself from bondage. I didn't want to have an attitude with my husband and I didn't want to view cooking, cleaning and being nice to my husband as servitude but I had been convinced of this for so long. The thought of being too "accessible" didn't sit well with me, until now. I knew my husband wasn't the type to take advantage of anyone at all, especially his wife. But regardless how much he showed me I did not have to worry about this, my deep-ridden subconscious thoughts made me feel a need to protect myself. If my husband's kind treatment and exceptional service to me wasn't convincing enough for me to drop those negative expectations and reform my thoughts, what else was there?

I was motivated to show as much care in serving my husband as he did serving me after giving birth. Once I got back on my feet, I envisioned myself taking care of everything regardless of how I stressed I was, not taking it out on him or trying my best not to let it show. I shouldn't put a damper on his mood because of whatever I was struggling with. But something happened, I had a high expectation but I didn't consider where I was mentally and how long it would take me to get to where I wanted to be. It's like going from C to Z in a week. No matter how much effort you exert, it's not going to happen! I needed to set milestones and draft out a plan, including how I can deal with getting back up when I fell, because it's not a matter of if you're going to fall, but when. So, after four and a half weeks of not doing any cleaning and cooking I abruptly went back to managing the household and taking care of a new born all at once. That can be pretty overwhelming for anyone, especially someone in my shoes who had already been struggling with time management and not letting my feelings reflect my service to my husband.

As a result, it wasn't long before I got overwhelmed and I was condemning myself for not being able to be the "perfect" Egyptian wife. Who made it obligatory for me to fulfill this standard? Not my husband for sure. He encouraged me to strive to be the best overall as a Muslim but he appreciated me for who I was; and why wouldn't he? After all, he knew who I was before he decided to marry me. However, I was still under the impression that the "Egyptian's way" of overdoing it was the ideal way a Muslim wife should be. This meant I was lacking in some type of way and fell behind and according to my knowledge, my background and upbringing prevented me from ever catching up. This was frustrating, always feeling like I had a deficiency and regardless of how much effort I put in, not feeling content with my level; I had no idea that I was the cause for my own anguish; since I was so busy condemning my past and using the Egyptian woman as a standard I couldn't appreciate where I was or see the beauty of what I went through.

But I was grateful for the progress I was able to make in having a better attitude with my spouse, in being timely in taking care of the chores and in having a healthier, more positive perspective in general. Yes, it was tough getting it all done but Alhumdulillah, Allah alleviated much difficulty from me when it came time to washing clothes. Allah upgraded us from the manual washer to a washer and spinner; this meant I no longer had the daunting task of empting out the contents after every wash and it eliminated rinsing the clothes and ringing each piece of clothing individually. That was a great relief. Also, we were really blessed us to do much better financially. We upgraded from eating meat only on the holidays to eating it once a week and sometimes even more frequently. And in no time we replaced boiling water with drinking filtered water from an expensive, irrigation filter system. We had money to go out and do things and we saved. Our Lord had really blessed us.

I painfully exerted myself in completing all the tasks of the day and entreated myself to keep working harder until I saw results. I was determined to do things better. I wanted to get to the point where I could check off the tasks at the end of the day instead of them constantly rolling over to the next day and slowing progress. I felt I didn't have the privilege of making time for myself and doing things that I enjoyed like writing, not until I fulfilled all my obligations without any deficiency or until everything was checked off completely. I wanted to fly but it seemed like I could never make leeway. As soon as I got into it, something else would come up and interrupt the flow of things. I breast fed the baby every two hours, so after nursing her for 45 minutes that only left me 1 hour and 15 minutes to get something done before going back to another feeding, not to mention changing, and other things that would always come up. I spent a countless amount of time trying to calculate what would be more time efficient. Should I start cooking a meal or sweep the floor? Should I throw a load of clothes in the wash machine or wash the dishes? I wanted to get it all done but sometimes had no idea where to start.

There were always things that needed to get done; I felt like I could never get a break. I could tell when Muhammad was annoyed; I knew he did not like when the house wasn't in order; it impeded his ability to function as it did for me as well. But he was patient and he helped out as much as he could, even with the escalating hours spent at work. I felt bad when he had to ask me to do something but I did not get to it due to my poor time management and inability to prioritize. Many times I would just slow down and feel tempted to give up. Everything needs to get done but regardless of what I do, at the end of the day some things won't get done, leaving me to go to bed with a weight and wake up with that same burden on my neck. Sometimes I delayed going to bed at a decent hour, seeking to at least get everything taken care of, but of course that would affect me getting a good night's rest and determine how early I was able to wake up. Even if I did come close to completing all the tasks, waking up late would put me behind again and I was back to square one. I reminded myself of women who were able to hold down the household, take care of the kids, plus more. Why wasn't I able to do that? I must be doing something wrong! But I had no idea what it was.

Every morning, I tried it again. I woke up early and started off with high motivation but by mid-day, when I saw things not going much different from the previous days I slowed down; not only did I begin to lose hope but I became exhausted. I had anemia which meant my blood doesn't carry enough oxygen to all the parts of my body, leaving my organs and tissues not working as well as they should. This meant it took me twice as much effort exerting myself than the average person, which left me getting tired quicker and in need of more time to recuperate and muster up the energy to get out there and try again. Shortly after giving birth I wasn't taking my pre-natal vitamins and iron pills regularly. I wasn't convinced that the low-cost pills offered in the drug store were effective so in time I stopped taking them all together. Not taking any measures to replace them, I would pay for it later on.

My husband was now working in Tonta and it took him four hours to travel every day. From the time he left the house in the morning until he came home at midnight, I was busy at work, looking forward to finishing up what I had to do so I could do a little bit of what I wanted to do. I had the entire day without having to stop my work to tend to my husband and still when he was getting home, often times I still couldn't check off all the items of the day. I was exhausted and not happy knowing that my husband had arrived and I hadn't even had sufficient time to unwind and do nearly as much as I wanted to. Needless to say, I wasn't that happy when my husband got home and I wasn't really in the mood to talk half the time but I pushed myself to have the best disposition that I could. When he asked me about my day, I refrained from complaining and asked him about his day. After working all day, I just wanted to sit down; I was exhausted! But I knew that he had been working all day too for both of us so I got up to offer his meal and make tea for him afterwards. I wish I had some down time for myself. I felt like I was being torn between my husband, my baby, and the countless chores and duties that kept coming up. I was drained and didn't know how much more I could take. I felt like all the pep was being drained from me.

School always motivated me and gave me a pep, but we still had not commenced after the long break. I noticed a decrease in my energy and need to push myself to get out of bed in the morning. I needed a major pick me up; some days I was more motivated than others. Depriving myself from including activities I enjoyed, many times I felt dead inside and asked myself what I had to look forward to. Needless to say, the enjoyment of being a mother had been sucked out of me and I came to dread all these "duties" that demanded my time and attention. I began to just go through the motions, living each day being confident that it wouldn't be any different than the previous ones. Hopefully school would start back up again soon.

By the grace of Allah, I did not allow my anguish to damper Muhammad's spirits. I was pleasant with him and I served him with a smile most of the times. The times I was really tested and was unable to be cheery with him, I was able to deal with him in a cordial way without taking my frustration out on him. I resisted the temptation to be dry and withdrawn with him and tried my best to treat him as I would want him to treat me. When he came home from work, I had dinner ready for him and was attentive. Our relationship had definitely improved drastically. Instead of arguing, we actually talked and I actually was beginning to enjoy his company like in the beginning. We had "video night" where we sat on the coach watched a lecture from someone knowledgeable such as a sheikh or a student of knowledge. Most times we popped some popcorn and made some tea to go along with the viewing.

I was accustomed to pedaling backwards for so long that it had become automatic. Now I faced the challenge of operating this device in the manner it was designed. I had to purify my mind of the poisonous thoughts and beliefs that had dictated my actions for so long and replace them with healthy, constructive ones so that I would actually move forward. It doesn't matter what I witnessed taking place in my parents' marriage or what anyone said or did. My husband was not my enemy and there was nothing wrong with serving him; it didn't mean I was going to go "overboard" with it like the Egyptians but I would be courageous enough to knock down the walls and try to be a little more open with him. It didn't mean I was subservient or less than; as a matter of fact it made me a humble servant of Allah and nothing could have elevated me to something greater.

I was motivated to go inward and embark on this wonderful transformation; no one else could do the work for me. There were times when I had to stop myself from falling into the same routine of pedaling backwards. There were times when pedaling the right way seemed strange, times when I slowed down and got discouraged but I kept on pedaling and asked God for assistance all the way.

Chapter 11

"You will never attain true faith until you want for your brother what you want for yourself." (Hadith or Saying of the Last Messenger, Sahih Bukhari & Sahih Muslim)

"I want you and the baby to come with me," my husband insisted.

I hesitated as I was sorting through the stacks of books in the living room.

I invited Jamillah to my house; she was a sister who had just made hijrah with her mother. This would be my second time meeting with her and I only got good vibes from her. She struck me as an innocent, sweet Muslimah who was striving to do what is pleasing to Allah. She was 19 years old, only 6 years younger than me.

I welcomed her to be herself. I had my hijab off and sat on the floor facing the sister, who sat on my couch. I offered her some fruit and some sweet tea and just talked to her. In the beginning, she shied away from accepting anything but after being at my house for at least an hour, she was comfortable enough to ask for more tea and she felt comfortable enough to have her hijab off as well; that's what I wanted, for her to be herself. We talked about marriage, Islam and just life in general. At the end of the conversation, I had confirmed my first impression about her.

"What do you think about polygamy?" I asked Jamillah.

"I love polygamy!" she answered.

This was the first time I heard anyone express so much enthusiasm for polygamy but I didn't think much of it at the time.

Then I asked her what she thought about marrying my husband. Within no time her face lit up; it was obvious the possibility of getting married excited her.

After inquiring about how she had been considered to marry my husband, I told her the story. She seemed really touched that I thought about her.

"Are you sure?" she asked me.

I took a moment to think about it again and then nodded my head in the affirmative.

"I really believe when you help other people, you help yourself," I told her.

I explained to her how this arrangement would also be beneficial to me being that I didn't want to move to Tonta.

"So I would be the one to move to Tonta?" she asked.

"Yes," I said without hesitation.

She expressed no resistance to moving and continued to articulate happiness for having the opportunity to do something she'd wanted to do for a while. I empathized with her; I recalled back to the years when I wanted to get married badly but wasn't so sure when or if it would actually happen.

She left my house smiling.

"Thank you," she told me again and gave me a hug. "I'm going to tell my mother."

A couple of days passed and I hadn't heard from her. The next time I spoke with her, she was asking if she could come over my house and ask me some questions.

"Sure," I said without thinking about it.

"When," she asked anxiously. "Monday?"

I wasn't sure if I'd be free as I was studying for exams. I had study sessions to attend, business I had to take care outside of the house and general studying. I was sure I had something planned on Monday but I made my intentions to postpone them for the sake of accommodating her.

"The only problem I have with your husband is I don't want to move to Tonta," she told me over the phone. I wasn't disappointed or mad. I didn't want to live in Tonta either.

Muhammad and I happened to be in the living room during the conversation with Jamillah over the phone. It was a Friday and we were enjoying each other's company in the living room. He was looking at a book and I was reclining on the couch, reviewing my notes from class.

After I relayed the news to him about Jamillah not wanting to move, he tensed up a bit.

"Nobody wants to move to Tonta," he said in a low tone, almost disappointed. I felt for him in his brief moment of dejection but I wasn't worried. I was confident everything would work out.

Then upon him leaving to make Salah in the Mosque, something incredible happened. I received an enlightened message that knocked me off my feet. While sitting down, I heard a firm voice order me to move to Tonta. I couldn't believe it. Not only that but it was coupled with a drumming in my heart; it was the same experience I had which let me know marrying my husband was the right thing to do, upon meeting him. I was 100% certain that this was coming from Allah. Where else would it be coming from? Certainly not from me; the last thing I wanted to do was move there. The feeling was so unadulterated; it was as if the words were inscribed in my heart, making me absolutely certain that living in Tonta was the best thing to do.

I was baffled. It doesn't make any sense, I thought to myself, trying to come to terms with it until I finally gave up. It's not for me to figure it out, I realized. Allah was guiding me to make a decision and look how far He has gotten me. Suddenly, I embraced the decision and loved the idea of sacrificing for the sake of Allah and being sure that Allah would compensate me. My husband told Jamillah that I was willing to move to Tonta and she was welcomed to inherit my residence in Alexandria. It felt so liberating totally giving everything to Allah and allowing Him to take care of all my affairs! So what if Jamillah went back on her agreement to move? There was no need for me to fight or protest. There was no doubt in my mind that when you follow the guidance from Allah, He makes all of your dealings smooth and in the end you end up getting what you need plus more!

"Babe, you need to apologize to her," my husband told me.

"She's the one who should be apologizing to me," I demanded, "for standing me up and playing games with me!"

Fajr time was approaching and my husband was on his way out to make Salah in the Masjid. I prayed, went inward and felt this humbleness come over me. Before my husband left the house I conceded to his suggestion and asked him to apologize to Jamillah on my behalf. He was on his way to have the first, official sit down with her and her wali after the dawn prayer to entertain the possibility of their marriage.

"Tell her I'm sorry for snapping at her on the phone," I said.

He would explain to her that I'm under a lot of stress studying for exams and when I kept rearranging my schedule to accommodate her and she didn't even give me the courtesy of a phone call, my patience began to wear.

That was part of it; I didn't tell him how she crossed the line, ruined a trust and altered the way I would now view her and for the sake of diffusing matters, I waged an internal jihad to forgive and forget and put her fowl treatment behind me. I tried to convince myself that she wasn't being haughty on purpose but with her making no attempt to acknowledge my apology, offer one of her own or at least explain herself made it difficult for me to think well of her or give her excuses.

I just could not believe this was the same sweet girl that I had gotten to know in the beginning. Maybe, that was the problem. I didn't know who she really was and how could I after having only a couple of conversations with her? What did I expect? This was a real eye opener and a lesson for all of eternity!

I felt this brewing animosity for Jamillah and a keen desire to give her a piece of my mind. How dare she play games, wrong me and have a nerve to be arrogant about it! The thing that really upset me was the lack of concern Jamillah showed for my feelings, the lack of consideration she showed for my time and the way she treated me. Ok, I reminded myself, this is a test. I struggled to overlook her faults and give her the benefit of the doubt, but boy was it an uphill battle!

Upon being in deep thought, I tried to figure out where things turned sour. She left my apartment smiling, then after not hearing from her in a couple of days, she was expressing doubt. Since then I have been adjusting my plans to accommodate her, and was repaid by getting disrespected.

An official sit down between my husband and Jamillah was put into motion where they would be allowed to ask each other questions and see if they were suitable for one another. But there seemed to be a huge miscommunication glitch; apparently, Jamillah, Muhammad and her wali all had different ideas of how things would go down and I would be left in the middle trying to enable messages between Jamillah and Muhammad.

Firstly, she needs to take a blood test, I told Muhammad. Good thing I said something because he seemed indifferent about the issue. He agreed but he was too laidback for my liking. Also, it was like Jamillah's wali was setting all the terms and Muhammad was just going with it, regardless of what we discussed beforehand. I understand that her wali has to play a major role and I didn't expect my opinion to be the most significant, but if certain things weren't squared away, there was going to be major problems occurring in me and my husband's marriage.

It's true…I had a chip on my shoulder. I felt bruised by Jamillah and hoped that the message my husband delivered to her would cause her to acknowledge her behavior and cause her to show concern in rectifying our relationship, but I was hoping for too much. Jamillah never made any attempt to patch up the sore wounds or show any genuine concern for our relationship as sisters in the deen.

I guess the fact that I didn't expect her to act in the way she did really threw me for a loop. I had nothing but good expectations of her but she started to show me another side. I became deeply troubled by the situation and what had happened; never had I felt so hurt and betrayed. I wanted her to feel the same pain that she caused me but I knew I couldn't allow my nafs to take over, so I resisted. I exerted all my efforts in being the bigger person and despite my battered emotional state, continued to treat her with kindness and respect. I prayed that Allah would forgive her and I made tawbah, seeking forgiveness for myself as well.

It was a painful exertion trying to stay committed to fruitful and positive thoughts, without getting sidetracked with my emotions. The distress of this feud growing between me and my future co-wife was daunting. This was the one thing that I hoped I would be spared from if I was in a polygamous marriage, and here I was on the brink of falling into a sea of misery and tension.

There's nothing that weighs a person more than having a spiteful relationship, especially with someone so close to home. If Jamillah and my husband got married and had children, they would be siblings to my children. Imagine the possible strain it would put on the children and their relationship with one another knowing the malevolence taking place between their mothers? As the older one, the one born into the deen and the first wife, I felt it was my responsibility to mend our relationship and the situation but a part of me felt like so much damage had been done. I hated the fact that we got started on the wrong foot and even if I tried my best to forgive her, I was starting to doubt how realistic it was for us to patch things up; I didn't feel safe around her and I didn't trust her. This made it even more of a struggle for me to refrain from spending too much thought on her or the situation; I didn't have the privilege of just forgetting about her and moving on with my life, because soon she would be a part of my life. If Allah willed, she would marry my husband, and I had to prepare myself for the major changes this would bring in my life.

I spent my days immersed in prayer, asking Allah to forgive me and soften my heart so I could forgive others. I went back to making istighfar throughout the day and began to be more sensitive about my sins and shortcomings. One of the best things that happened as a result of this trial was me returning to Allah in repentance in a more gracious manner than ever before.

Chapter 12

"And I free not myself (from the blame). Verily, the self is inclined to evil, except when my Lord bestows His mercy. Verily, my Lord is Oft- Forgiving, Most Merciful." (Qur'an 12:53)

I had a bitter taste in my mouth about what happened between me and Jamillah but still hoped we would be able to repair our relationship as sisters in Islam, regardless of what happened with her and my husband.

When Muhammad came home from the sit-down with Jamillah and told me about a contract that would be drawn between them the following week, I nearly flew into a rage.

"This isn't what we agreed on," I reminded him. "What about the blood test and you getting the apartment before marrying her." Since he didn't get the apartment in Tonta yet, I feared she would invite herself to my home and attempt to hang out there; given what she showed me, I didn't put it pass her. She already had a way of pushing my buttons; I could imagine her showing up at our home and doing all types of stuff to get under my skin. I was getting agitated by the minute thinking about everything that was taking place. My husband was not a passive person but he was just allowing Jamillah's wali to dictate everything that would take place and I wasn't going for it. I made it clear that I was not happy with the way things were going and I wasn't budging on the two main issues: her taking a blood test and him getting the place in Tonta before the marriage.

Muhammad quietly listened to me and then called her wali to tell him that he will not marry her until he gets the apartment in Tonta. I had to go to the bathroom to cool off; I hadn't remembered feeling anger like that in a long, long time. I could not believe I allowed Shaytan to manipulate my emotions and cause me to go off like that.

I couldn't turn off my emotions: the rage, anxiousness and most of all, fear had too much control over me. I was afraid that my husband's and my marriage would go downhill from this point, and that it may not even survive. What's more, I feared that Jamillah would bring out the worse in me and cause me to end up lashing out at her because of her immature and insensitive behavior. What did I get myself into? I thought. I did not see this coming! My husband was making plans to marry this other woman and the dynamics of our marriage would change forever.

"Could you ask your husband to come to my house," Jamillah asked with an attitude, "because I have another question to ask him." This girl really has some nerve, I thought to myself. This was the first time we had spoken since the last incident over the phone, and she didn't feel compelled to excuse herself for her past actions or even acknowledge the message I sent to her by my husband. In fact, she showed no concern to clear up any possible misunderstanding or neutralize the "bad blood" that had thickened between us. Yet the news of Muhammad delaying marrying her motivated her to call me right away and break the silence between us.

Her proud attitude and lack of regard for her actions intensified the overwhelming distaste I had for her and her character.

I took a moment to compose myself. "He's not home right now but I can call him and ask if he can meet you tomorrow," I told her without losing my cool.

Then after calling him and confirming that he could do it, I called her back to give her the time he was available. "He can meet you after shuruq."

"What?!" she asked with conceit, clearly not knowing what the word shuruq meant.

"About an hour or so after Fajr."

And that was it.

But as Allah would have it, her mother's trip out of town would put a monkey wrench in her plans. A couple of minutes later I got another phone call from Jamillah. Though she had a really bad attitude the previous times I talked to her, I did not let it prevent me from treating her in the same courteous manner in which I've been dealing her from day one. I gave her the proper greeting, as cheerful as if I were greeting a friend who I was happy to hear from. She would respond like an immature school girl, hurriedly replying as if the greeting was something she had to get over with before getting to her agenda.

Every time she called, I tried it again.

"As salamu alaikum," I answered the phone pleasantly.

This time her voice resembled that of one humbled.

"How are you?" I asked, following the same protocol I always did.

"I'm fine," she said. "How are you?"

"Alhumdulillah," I answered.

"My mother and her husband are going to Cairo tomorrow so we're not going to be able to meet," she said.

Look at that, I thought to myself.

Then for the next couple of minutes she was trying to devise a plan so that she could meet with me and Muhammad.

"I don't know if you think it's appropriate or not but maybe I can come to your house?" she boldly asked.

I got straight to the point. "What's this about, the marriage contract?"

She hesitated, clearly shocked that I had gotten to the point so quickly. "Uh, yeah. I thought it was going to be next week?!" she asked.

Whatever it is she wanted to accomplish, she was really serious about it. At the end of that conversation, I was sure of the importance of using caution when dealing with her.

"I'll ask him when he gets in and we'll get back to you."

I thought back to when she was in my apartment and she briefly told me about an altercation between her and her former co-wife, shortly after Jamillah had married her husband. From the way she told the story, her husband's first wife was the aggressor, but I realized that there is always two sides to a story. She didn't even marry my husband yet and I was already battling my emotions, so who knows what kind of drama that other sister went through after Jamillah married her husband. It doesn't justify the first wife coming to her house and starting drama, if in fact she did that; but if she kept provoking me the way she did, especially after marrying my husband, I would be tempted to teach her a lesson.

There were certain things I would not tolerate. I would not tolerate her coming to my house unannounced and I would not tolerate her making demands to see her husband and refusing to leave when politely asked. Of course she didn't do that and they weren't even married yet but I could predict her doing all kinds of things to get attention. She already admitted that she was jealous and insecure but I didn't think much of it because we all feel jealousy once in a while. But there is a difference between a person who tries to control feelings of jealousy and an insecure and jealous person who fails to control their nafs; the latter will always be disastrous because there is little or no reminder about Allah and the consequences of their actions.

I think now I figured out why she said she loved polygamy; it's not that she necessarily loved polygamy but it's coming in as the second wife that enthused her. If she's the jealous and insecure person that she admits to being, then she lacks the confidence of being able to maintain her husband's interest and love. However, if she comes in as second, she has the ability to grab her husband's attention, particularly when things are bland between him and his first wife, and become the prized possession. Perhaps she concluded that a man seeking another wife was not content in his marriage. But she was wrong; not every man interested in polygamy is bored, unsatisfied or searching for something else and I had proof. Jamillah wasn't able to come in during a train wreck and put the pieces together because a strong foundation was built and we were continuing to build, with the permission of Allah. Little did she know, my husband and I were more than just husband and wife, we were close friends.

When Muhammad came home from work, I was disturbed, withdrawn and unable to give him a smile or ask him about his day. Without him even having to inquire what was wrong, he picked up on my being perturbed and began to feel compassion for me. He noticed what the situation was doing to me and it started to trouble him as well.

I was trying so hard not to be consumed by emotions but it was taking a toll on me. I found myself so mentally fatigued that I was no longer compelled to engage in cheery conversation. My mind was absent in almost every task that I took up. When I cooked, cleaned or fed my daughter, I likened it to a ritualistic routine.

I sat down and grabbed a paper and pen. My husband knew what that meant. When I felt clogged, I secluded myself from everyone and everything in my life, attempted to go inward and address whatever emotions I was feeling. Seeing me in that state prompted my husband to pick up a paper and pen also.

"I'm going to write the sister a letter," he said and in a brief letter, he told her very firmly, there's no need to rush getting married because there's some things that need to get ironed out. First, she has to get a blood test. Then he admonished her, saying "if it's your intention to test us, I'm advising you not to do so because you're not qualified to do so." And he ended it off by requesting her…"please don't turn this into a burden."

He read the letter to me, from start to finish and once he got my approval, sent it with her little brother to give to her. I felt good knowing he was stepping up and making sure the things we agreed on would be implemented for the betterment of all parties involved. I felt confident that if he practiced polygamy he would do it the right way. It wasn't him I was worried about, it was the fitnah of the incoming party that kept me up at night.

Jamillah wouldn't let up. As soon as she received the letter from my husband, she was now passing messages on to her brother to tell Muhammad that she wanted to meet. I was starting to get tired of hearing her name; every time you turn around there was something else. She was stressing to meet as if it was urgent and at the rate she wanted to meet, it seemed as if she didn't have much to do with her time. Did she want everyone to stop what they were doing and meet with her in an instant if she requested so?

The demands in my life were constantly tugging on me; I had no time to waste on petty matters that would threaten my peace of mind even further. I was a wife, mother, student and a hafiz in the making, with the permission of Allah. I saw her as impeding on my time and space and wished she would take it easy. I understood she wanted to get married badly but she didn't realize what this was doing to me; this was a huge adjustment for me and I didn't want to feel like I was being cornered and forced to deal with this when I wasn't emotionally stable. It took all the discipline that I could conjure to restrain myself from lashing out at her and to deal with her in the same respectful manner that I did with everyone else. I kept praying for her and kept fighting my negative feelings, and I felt stronger and more connected to Allah each time I sought refuge in Him.

"I can meet with her after I finish with my exams," I told my husband, "so if she really wants to meet with me, then she'll have to wait."

I was done breaking my neck to accommodate her; it was crunch time and if I didn't zero in on my studies, I would only have myself to blame. Besides, something told me chatting with me wasn't at the top of her priority list; after all, how much time did she have to reach out to me before the letter incident, yet all she could talk to me about was wishing to meet my husband. But still, I gave her the benefit of the doubt; after all only Allah knows what's hidden in our hearts.

I was friends with Jamillah's mother; she was a lovely sister who was friendly and easy to talk with. I called her and Jamillah happened to pick up the phone.

"What are you doing today?" Jamillah asked nonchalantly as if we were buddies.

"I have some business to take care of," I said dryly. She had to know that I wasn't going to just drop everything and meet her on demand like that, not anymore.

Then I offered clemency and initiated meeting with her, without her even having to ask. It was obvious she wanted to talk; I wasn't going to make it harder on her. After eating a little humble pie, I Imagined her reflecting and learning her lesson by now.

"I'm pretty busy but I'm available Monday if you want to meet."

"What time?" she asked.

"How about the morning?" I knew she usually didn't get her day started until the afternoon but with my hectic schedule, the best thing for me was to get it over with in the morning so that I could move on with my day.

"What time in the morning," she asked inquisitively. From the way she said it, I knew she wasn't enthusiastic about meeting early in the morning. Of course she made the meetings with my husband after Fajr because that was the best time he could meet, but if she had a choice, if she didn't have to get out of bed so early, she wouldn't.

I let out a friendly laugh and Jamillah joined in with me. We ended on a good note. It seems like things were off to a better start. I was happy about that. I was willing to compromise. I knew she wasn't a morning person.

"I tell you what, we'll confirm beforehand and decide on a time."

I got off the phone feeling light. I was willing to give her another chance and start on a clean slate. But the events that would take place over the next couple of days would have me on an emotional roller coaster and have me wondering me what I got myself into.

I was crying in my Salah thanking Allah for postponing the marriage contract that would be drawn up for Jamillah and my husband. In the wake of Muhammad taking the initiative to meet with Jamillah to see why she wanted to meet so badly, he came back with information that I wasn't ready to hear. I couldn't believe what she said out of her mouth! The more I got to know her, the more I realized she was nothing like I'd perceived her to be. I wasn't so sure I wanted her marrying my husband anymore and if so, I didn't know how long my marriage would survive. I was shocked and terribly disgusted at what I learned. What was her intention in wanting to meet? Was it so she could get him to feel sorry for her, manipulate him and convince him to marry her sooner? I didn't want to believe that but I couldn't figure out why she told him what she did. Muhammad, having the kind nature that he did, didn't suspect her as being fraudulent. I refrained from being suspicious but kept my qualms to myself and continued to make calculations. As an objective person, looking at the situation from the outside, I was able to see that it did not add up.

That was the longest and most passion-filled Salah I ever recall making; I just cried out to Allah hysterically, unable to stop while reciting the Qur'an. I couldn't show enough gratitude to Allah.

"Thank you, Allah! Thank you!" I cried out.

I managed to re-focus and get my last bit of studying in for exams. I was still bothered about the recent information I learned but continued to pray and do my best to stay on task. Once I finished taking my exams, I exhaled and was able to relax a little more.

"Tell Jamillah if she still wants to meet tomorrow, she can come at 12:00 p.m. If she doesn't want to meet anymore, it's okay, just ask her to give me a call and let me know so that I'm not waiting for her. Sometimes I have to leave the house and run errands," I told her little brother.

It was the day before Monday, the day we had agreed to meet. But now that she had already met with Muhammad and they were back on good terms again, I wasn't so sure if she was still interested in meeting with me any longer.

"Allah, please send me a sign if she's sincere or not. If she's not sincere, don't allow her to come here to my house today," I prayed.

The appointed time came. It was Monday at 12:00 and no sign of Jamillah. Maybe, she woke up late, I thought to myself. I'll give her respite. I continued to take care of things I needed to get done in the house. I wasn't annoyed at all. I purposely picked a day in which I wouldn't have to take care of any urgent matters out of the house and since I was finished studying for my exams, I wasn't allowing her to steal precious studying time from me. I looked at the clock from time to time but I never stopped what I was doing. I remained focused on taking care of business as if I hadn't expected a visitor. I wasn't going to call her or question her. I didn't think I was asking too much when I requested that she show courtesy to me and my time, but if she didn't feel a need to, then that's between her and Allah. At a certain point I stopped checking the clock all together and no longer battled feelings of irritation like I did in the past because I was completely contented. I was jubilant with the idea of not allowing her to stress me anymore; I had taken too much on my shoulders and it wasn't healthy for me. The idea of it being dissolved put me at ease. It was time for me to move on with my life. It was 10 p.m.

and Jamillah never came to my house and she didn't call to excuse herself or give any explanations. I never called her and went to bed feeling at rest.

"As salamu alaikum, is Jamillah awake?" I asked her mother on the phone, the next day.

"No, she's still sleeping."

"It's okay, you don't have to wake her. I have a gift for her. I'll just leave it with her brother."

Jamillah's brother met me to retrieve the gift.

"Did you give Jamillah the message?" I asked him. "Did you ask her to call me and let me know if she could not make it?"

"Yes," he said.

"Okay, I just wanted to confirm she got the message."

I gave him the gift; it was a notebook with a note in it encouraging her not to give up. I told her that I find writing very helpful and I urged her to write her feelings and experiences, as a means of therapy. I happily signed it: your sister in Islam. I had intended to give the journal to her when she came to my home, so I figured I'd give it to her now.

In addition, she got another surprise; it was a letter from my husband. Inside the letter, it said: "I can't marry you."

Within a couple of minutes after giving the notebook and the letter to her brother, Jamillah was calling my phone. I didn't answer.

My husband and I had a day of fun and fish. He took me to visit some friends and we celebrated moving on with our marriage without the extra baggage. Yes, it was official; he broke off all ties with the sister and from that day on our relationship improved, even better than before Jamillah was in the picture. Allah is truly the Greatest!

Chapter 13

**"Surely, your Lord is Allah who created the heavens
and the earth in six days and then istawa (rose above)
the throne (in a matter that suits His majesty), disposing
the affairs of all things. No intercessor (can plead with
Him) except after His leave. That is Allah, your Lord;
so worship Him (alone). Then will you not remember?"
(Qur'an 10: 3)**

Moving to Tonta was an exciting experience! I looked
forward to the new change, new town, meeting new friends
and new experiences. I spent most of the two hour train
ride, looking out the window, appreciating Allah's
beautiful creation. I didn't have a school lined up yet, but I
would just have to be patient. I was blessed to find the
school in Alexandria; He could replace me with something
better, easily.

I visited the wife of one of Muhammad's friends. She was one of the few African Americans I met since coming to Egypt. She was down to earth, funny and easy to talk with. I met her friend, who happened to be doing her daughter's hair that day. She was friendly and had a warm spirit about her. I could tell by the way she and the host interacted, they were very good friends.

"I breast-fed all of them," my hostess said proudly, referring to her co-wife's children.

The sister who was doing her daughter's hair was also her co-wife and they had the most beautiful friendship ever. They happily co-existed and helped each other on a daily basis. After one gave birth, the other cooked for her and after one had surgery, the other gave up her days with her husband so that he could assist her during her time of difficulty. My heart melted. This is the type of relationship I envisioned having with my co-wife if I were to be involved in a polygamous relationship, and since things were going in the opposite direction, I continuously thanked Allah for saving me from that trial. Though I conceded to polygamy, Allah knows what each of us can and can't handle. I just thank Him for allowing me to learn the lesson without having to be put through the ringer. My negative experience did not make me view polygamy in a deleterious way. Polygamy itself has many benefits but some people are not mature enough to take part in it and thus they tarnish the idea of two or more women being married to the same man.

I was so proud of the maturity, compassion and respect exhibited by my two new friends. They had different personalities but I loved them and appreciated them as individuals. They lived in separate quarters but in the same apartment building which made it very convenient for them to visit one another daily. There was a constant revolving door of their children going in and out of the front door, some of which paired up to attend class together. The husband spent two days at one's house and two days at another's house and gave each of them the respect of not seeing, talking to or mentioning the other one when it wasn't her turn.

"My co-wife nor I know where our husband's heart lies. When he's with me, he's with me and when he's with her, he's with her."

I smiled. "May Allah continue to bless you guys," I told her.

I realized the way the husband dealt with and treated his wives was the key. Being that the women are in such a vulnerable state, what the husband did or didn't do could make the difference between night and day. He could be fueling enmity and jealousy between them without even knowing it. Naturally both wives would want to be the one more beloved to the husband and by him showing more affection to one or showing more enthusiasm to be with one or casting another to the side could not only affect the wife's self-esteem but also cause her to breed feelings of resentment, jealousy and hatred towards her co-wife. Polygamy is no cake walk; it's a very delicate situation and all parties must be qualified to deal with it. Sometimes the man thinks he is capable of handling it but in the process ruins both marriages and leaves a bad taste in the children's mouths. In some cases it can be so destructive that the impression that they get from their parents' marriage affects them for life. Look at what happened to me.

If marriage between two people takes work, those involved in a plural marriage had better be prepared to roll up their sleeves. But it can be done and seeing the beautiful way my two new friends were able to work together peacefully without the drama, jealousy, or spite made me feel good knowing there are people out there who are benefitting from something that Allah has allowed for a reason. Women continue to outnumber men and with things such as a high number of male incarceration rate, especially in the Black community, polygamy facilitates many women to get married, who would otherwise have the option of being alone for the rest of their lives or do something many women in the West would admit to: taking matters in their own hands by having an affair with a man already taken or attempt to take him away from his spouse. The stealth of this when compared to the honesty of a legitimate marriage to more than one woman and having children who are not bastards and unaccounted for, makes polygamy seem more advantageous. Still, anyone who rushes into polygamy without having the discipline and without thinking it through and planning may cause more devastation than good. It is a serious decision that should propel one to be very honest with him or herself about their capabilities before delving into a matter that must be taken with care.

Some would have imagined the drama taking place between me and the sister who almost married my husband to affect our relationship in a negative way but Allah can make anything happen. It was a gift from Allah because He strengthened the bond between me and my husband. Being in that situation tested our relationship and caused it to become stronger. It was during that time when he was planning to marry her that caused him to share something with me that he never did before; Allah guided him to be honest with me and completely open up the doors of communication to a whole other level. As a result our relationship improved in a multitude of ways in addition to our appreciation for one another.

We spent more quality time together and at one point I was actually looking forward to him coming home. He ate, shared with me any interesting or funny events of the day and we just talked. I enjoyed his company and his peculiar sense of humor. From the serious impression that people got of him, no one would have ever guessed how much he made me laugh in the home. And he was able to do it without even trying; since he knew me so well, it was easy for him to know what tickled me. I really believed he enjoyed making me have a good laugh; there were times when I was on the floor from uncontrollable laughter and he continued to crack me up.

There was nothing more valuable than having a mate who knew me so well and cared enough to consider my emotions. When he saw I was disturbed, annoyed, or upset, he would stop whatever he was doing and try everything to comfort me and wouldn't leave me until he saw a smile. I really appreciated that; this showed me that there wasn't anything worth doing if his wife wasn't okay. Making sure his other half was stable and there was peace in the home was a priority to him. This held great weight with me and softened my heart a great deal when my heart was in need of it most.

Muhammad and I virtually stopped arguing. I learned to be patient and listen to him, without cutting him off, though at times I did slip when I really wanted to get my point across. Still, the times I was convinced I was right, I had a new attitude. I sincerely tried to look at the situation so that we could come to a resolution. This felt much better than trying to battle him and over-speak him, only to feel guilty in the end. Now, I was able to not get too upset because I was beginning to look at the bigger picture. So what if I lose an argument, that's much easier than losing my husband's respect. And what's the point of being right if you're not happy. In time I learned that me being fierce with my husband and trying to get him to see my point wasn't wise; it was exhausting, time-consuming and it brought little good, if any at all. I began to enjoy taking a chill pill, being humble and listening more. Maybe there was a misunderstanding somewhere.

Maybe if I listened more and talked less, I could see where there was a breakdown in communication. In addition, I began to view the way I serve my husband in a different light. I recalled a time when I would delay praying Esha up until my husband came home so I would have an excuse from serving his dinner or giving him something to drink. I knew that he wasn't going to wait until I finished praying to ask me to serve him as some husbands do who "can't do anything in the kitchen." He would just fix his own meal and make his own tea, thereby relieving me from feeling like the "slave" who has to do something. Later on I realized how horrible this was of me. I was only shortchanging my own self by losing out on the blessings but being at the place where I was, no one could have convinced me of this. It was something I had to learn on my own and by struggling against my nafs, changing the way I thought, and by praying a lot, in time I began to become much happier with myself, my husband, and my life, and felt at peace. Initially, I couldn't understand the significance of women going to the kitchen to get something for their husbands, when they could get it themselves, but in time I got the answer. I knew why.

Chapter 14

"You are only a warner." (35:23)

"Abdul Hakim's getting married today!" my husband alerted me in alarm over the phone.

"Are you serious?!"

"Yeah, I'm trying to call him but I can't get in contact with him," Muhammad said anxiously.

There was nothing I could do but I felt flattered that he chose to call me to seek comfort. After all, I was his friend.

He was concerned about Abdul Hakim's welfare. He was going to marry Jamillah, the same girl he almost married. Abdul Hakim came to Muhammad only a couple of days prior because he was warned about marrying the sister. He inquired my husband about it, knowing that he almost married her. In a very vague way, without exposing the sister's dirty laundry, Muhammad strongly advised his friend against marrying her, simply asking him if he wants to be married to someone who is dishonest. Still, the brother needed details and once he saw my husband wasn't going to say much more, he stopped. "She should tell you," Muhammad said.

Then he advised him to speak to Yasin, another brother she almost married but didn't because of fitnah that she initiated between her and his wife, who had opened her arms to her and welcomed her even after she sent hints that she was interested in her husband. In fact, it was due to Yasin's wife telling her that she didn't mind her marrying her husband that her husband even considered taking her as a second wife. Once Yasin witnessed the behavior of Jamillah, he cut the ties with her before even having a sit down.

"Did Abdul Hakim talk to you like I told him to do?" My husband asked Yasin.

"No," Yasin responded.

Instead of taking the advice of someone who knew the sister and doing a background check, he proceeded to marry the girl, without inviting Muhammad or Yasin to the wedding. Abdul Hakim already had two wives and the information that he didn't know about her could not only jeopardize his health but his wives' as well.

It was only hours until the wedding would take place. Muhammad kept trying to reach Abdul Hakim until he finally got through.

"Listen, did the sister tell you about her condition?" My husband asked her.

"No," Abdul Hakim said, clueless.

"She has a disease and it's not curable."

"I'll call you back," Abdul Hakim said, hurrying off the phone.

Only Allah knows what conversation took place between Abdul Hakim and Jamillah but the next day Abdul Hakim no longer looked at Muhammad in the same friendly way that he always did but stood with his arms folded, sizing him up. He looked at him suspiciously as if he was trying to discern the truth.

"What's this about this disease?"

"We're talking about a STD here," Muhammad told him.

Abdul Hakim wanted to know exactly what it was but Muhammad didn't want to reveal any of the sister's faults. But when it became clear that he wasn't letting up, he gave in.

"What is it?"

When my husband finally told him the STD that his wife had, he nearly lost his mind.

"I seek refuge in Allah from the evil of Shaytan!" the brother screamed out in distress.

It was too late. He already married her, on the same day my husband called him to give him the news about her condition.

"I hate to be the bearer of bad news," Muhammad said compassionately. "Let me know if you need anything."

It was nothing like seeing up close and personal the disaster that would have befallen me and my husband had not Allah showered his grace upon us and exposed the sister before Muhammad made the commitment of marrying her. He was this close to being persuaded into marrying her right away and this close to doing it without having taken a blood test.

"Marriage is something you're not supposed to delay," I recall the brothers telling my husband, in an effort to get him to marry the girl right away.

This may be the case but a polygamous situation is something you have to plan for and if you fail to do so, the results can be disastrous. Look at this case here. Not only did the brother jeopardize himself but he jeopardized the women who he was married to because of haste and stubbornness in doing what he wanted despite the signs sent to him.

Chapter 15

"Or think you that you will enter Paradise without such (trials) as came to those who passed away before you? They were afflicted with severe Poverty, Ailments & were Shaken." (Qur'an 2:214)

The riots in Egypt spread and the instability of the government declined along with the order and stability of the country. My family was alarmed! The fear that my parents would never see their daughter and their granddaughter, who they had yet to meet, became more ostensible. My parents doubled teamed me and called me from the States to petition us to come back but we couldn't even if we wanted to. The baby didn't have her passport and due to the conditions, the U.S. Embassy was shut down. It was reported that all Americans were highly encouraged to leave the country. Almost every time you turned around, we heard of more Americans returning back to the U.S., even those Muslim Americans who intended to make hijrah and adopt Egypt as their new home, as we did.

But as conditions worsened, we realized the importance, now more than ever, to establish and maintain a deep connection with Allah; for only our Lord could foresee what was ahead and grant us the protection and guidance we so desperately needed.

My baby hadn't even made it to her first year before I found myself pregnant again. Allah is the best of the planners I reminded myself, trying to see the silver lining. I felt exhausted, overwhelmed and fragile as ever but still I tried to push through with every effort to make it day by day. I couldn't find a steady flow in taking care of my baby, managing the house, completing a million and one chores that came in between, not to mention trying to attend to the needs of my husband, forget it. The spontaneity was sucked out of my life and I was deprived of the ability of going here and there, by myself, as I pleased. Due to the instability of the country, we needed to take security measures and it wasn't safe for me to go out with the baby alone. I understood this was necessary for me and the baby's security but I hated it. I felt inhibited and I had nothing to look forward to; I still wasn't able to find a school yet to give me something purposeful outside of the mundane housework, in addition to aiding my mind with the mental stimulation and challenge it needed to thrive. Muhammad's day at work became increasingly longer which limited the help he could offer in the house. Still, he incorporated it in his routine to help me as much as he could. Before he left for work he took the baby out of the crib and put her in a make-shift play pin he had set up in the front room, near the window. This way, the baby would get vitamin D from the sunlight that beamed through the living room windows. If it wasn't for my husband doing this practice, my poor daughter would have stayed there in the crib, deprived of sunlight and food because by the time I woke up I was so backed up with a list of things to do and had no idea where to start. By the time I fully woke up, I had to make sure I prayed Salatul Zhur before it went out, eat to give myself some energy, have some food prepared for my husband to take with him to work, make sure his outfit was ironed if it wasn't already, and be available to assist him in getting out the house, if needed.

I became increasingly guilty for not making breakfast for my husband in the morning. Most of the time, by the time I woke up, usually late in the afternoon, he had already eaten, fed the baby and was on his way out the door for work. On some occasions, I attempted to assist him in getting things ready for work, but waking up in a state of confusion and bewilderment and not knowing where to start, left me severely limited in assisting him, my baby, and even myself for that matter.

"Do I have any clothes?" Muhammad asked.

It took me a while to recollect my thoughts and understand what he was asking.

I hit my forehead with the palm of my hand. He was getting ready for work and I had forgotten to iron his clothes again.

"That's all right, he said calmly, looking through the closet for the least wrinkled outfit to wear. How many times must he do this before you get it together, I asked myself, beating up on myself. I didn't have a system for keeping up with his clothes, the chores or the baby and I didn't have a clue on how to develop one. I intended to get it all done, telling myself: today is going to be better. But the moment things fell apart, I retreated, feeling disappointed and frustrated. I felt like a failure to myself and my husband, not to mention my daughter who got her needs met only when I had the ability to dig deep for the strength and will power. I had no activities for her, I wasn't talking to her, reading to her or encouraging her to crawl or pull up on the crib. She, like her mother, soon became lifeless, just sitting in the crib, with nothing much to look forward to. How can I have another child? I can barely take care of this one. What will happen to me after I have this baby, I worried inwardly. Yes, it definitely was a blessing but I wanted to make sure I was in a state where I could receive it as such. I was in turmoil and didn't know where to turn. I continued praying to Allah; I knew He had the answers, I just had to be patient.

"Are you going to welcome your new neighbor?" my husband asked me.

I paused for a moment. No one moved into the building except his friend, Abdul Hakim, who was accompanied with his new wife, Jamillah.

As we know, the Prophet Muhammad (SAW) stressed kind treatment to your neighbors and relayed to us the astronomical rewards for having such conduct. I had become more accustomed to offering food and treats to neighbors and trying to show as much acts of kindness as I could to them and really enjoyed it. I had a good relationship with all of my neighbors and it was always an exchange of good vibes and mutual well-wishing.

However, my interactions with Jamillah have had the opposite effect. She was known to start fitnah, even with those who treated her kindly. I learned that a lot of people were angry with her and it seemed as if she wasn't the least bit concerned at all; if I didn't know any better I would have thought she had a disease of the heart because her actions testified that she enjoyed hurting people and doing everything she could to get under people's skin.

I forgave Jamillah but had always used caution being around her because I wasn't sure what she was capable of; I didn't quite trust her and I wasn't sure if it was wise to be around her at all. A part of me thought maybe I should just leave where we left off, on a good note, rather than risk bad blood being bolt once again.

"Good can only come from good," my husband would say. His philosophy was you can't lose by being kind, regardless of the results or response from others. I agreed to a certain extent. I was the type who kept my distance unless I was absolutely sure that the other side would respond positively. Otherwise, if I received any signs that someone didn't want to be bothered, I wouldn't even make an attempt to approach them, even if there was an inkling of good coming from it. However, my husband challenged me to get out of my box and open myself up to more blessings. I always thought he had a purer heart than mine. He was able to turn the other cheek and be good to the same person who wronged him without even thinking about it. On the other hand, for me it was a process! It took hard work and much effort! Alhumdulillah, I was willing to go through it because I knew it was beneficial, but I was always careful about not putting myself in a position where I could get hurt. Even if it involves good, if there was a possibility of me feeling slighted and getting hurt, that was a big deal and I had to think about if it was worth it. My husband was the type that would profit by stacking up his scale of blessings by partaking in the same good deeds that people like me gave up by sitting there thinking about it.

"This is a race for good deeds," he would remind me but with me and my stubborn ways, it took a while for this concept to sink in. But once I was willing to take the risk of stepping out there and imparting kindness to others without allowing the fear of people's responses to interfere, it has proved to be the most phenomenal experience for me.

I just wasn't sure if it was the wise thing to do in this situation. I wanted to believe that Jamillah had grown since the experience we shared, but I had to be prepared that she was the same person with the same ways. I wanted to protect myself from any possible harm and avoid any possible fitnah.

Not long after my husband had cut ties with her, I saw her at the Masjid. This was when we were still living in Alexandria, not long after the incident where she stood me up. At that moment when she saw me face to face, I sensed her apprehension in not knowing how to respond or react to me. She had attempted to call my phone but I didn't answer, and she had no idea why. For all she knew, I could have been pissed off at her and was waiting to see her in person so I could roast her or embarrass her in front of everyone. Would I put her on the hot seat and question her about what happened, causing her to search for excuses and stutter? Would I expose her faults to everyone and rally everyone to turn against her?

Although I was tempted to question her about the last incident, I decided against it. I didn't expose her faults or embarrass her, and I made no attempt to rally the people against her or even broadcast that she harmed me. I refrained from putting her in the hot seat or even bringing up the incident at all.

Instead, I embraced her with a big hug and sincere greetings. I asked her how she was and continued on my path. I knew I made the right decision. It felt good choosing the higher road and I was confident that Allah would repay me by giving me more than a brief satisfaction of seeing her squirm. It was over and I was able to forgive her and move on with my life.

Jamillah opened the door, seemingly happy to see my face.

"I'm not going to stay. I just wanted to give you this," I told her. It was a plate of chicken stew. She thanked me and I was on my way. That was easy, I thought to myself. Kindness doesn't cost anything but it's the most needed thing in the world; it softens hearts and inspires people to confer the same kindness upon others. Most of the time the person least deserving of kindness is in need of it the most.

Something astounding happened when I came back to the apartment. The lethargic and dead feeling I had previous to the trip had disappeared. I now felt light and happy. This act of kindness not only helped my neighbor but it helped me. I couldn't believe how such a small act could impact me in such a huge way. By simply doing a selfless act for someone else, without expecting anything in return, I was benefitting from it as well. The good response that I got from her and lack of fitnah encouraged me to increase in seeking good deeds.

This didn't mean I was suddenly her best friend. I didn't visit her every day, but was merely conscious of helping her in any way that I could. I learned that I could develop a relationship with her without getting too close, thereby protecting myself from any possible harm. I gave her the benefit of the doubt, but I didn't put myself in a position where I would be vulnerable to receive harm from her. I never told her my business, never asked her for anything and I was the one who came to her house to drop off items; she didn't come to mine. In time, she began to feel more comfortable with me and I even noticed her beginning to offer to share food with me. This shocked me since I never expected her to return any favors. However, I was beginning to see that maybe Allah was using me as an example for her and who knows, maybe she had turned over a new leaf. If so, who knows of the enormous rewards awarded to me for being patient with her and daring to deal with her with rahmah.

The elated feeling I got through being pleasant to Jamillah was wholesome, but it was going to take more than a couple of acts of kindness to transform my condition. I was in a hole. I had to convince myself to get out of bed each day, and when I was up, I dragged my feet to take care of things, with lost hope that the day would be better than the previous ones. I failed in keeping the house tidy, in taking care of the baby sufficiently and taking care of myself. I walked around with dumpy clothes, undone hair and no desire to do better. I just accepted that things would continue to roll over to the next day and made no real effort to getting them under control.

I fell into severe depression. I woke up later and later, and only got up when it was time to offer obligatory prayers. I struggled against my nafs to get up, but Alhumdulillah, I was able to offer my Salah. I was tempted to fall back to sleep and if it wasn't for my baby I would have. Your baby needs you, I told myself. Then I had to wash her, change her and be there for her but with no motivation to live life, this meant exerting twice the effort. I knew she needed more. She needed her mother, but mentally I wasn't there.

Just making wudu exerted so much effort. Okay, you can do it, I convinced myself and made myself fulfill the necessary rituals until the next time. Knowing that prayer was beneficial for me, especially during this time, was the only thing that got me through.

I sat there on the bathroom stall for almost half an hour, twisting my hair, thinking, praying for strength, and trying to convince myself to get up so I could take care of what I had to take care of. But it was hard to level with myself. It's not like I could tell myself, just take care of these things and then you can do what you'd like to do. I knew that would never be the case. No matter how much I tried, I would always be behind schedule and would always be left doing things that I had to do, never having any time for the things I wanted to do. Life became a barrage of never-ending responsibilities and monotonous, boredom-filled days.

I wanted life to be over with but wasn't senseless enough to even attempt taking it. I knew I was suffering now; I didn't want to make matters drastically worse by being dragged into Hell and being condemned to a painful torment for eternity.

"Allah doesn't give us more than we can handle," I reminded myself. "Allah is with the patient."

I tried to remind myself to just be patient and that this would pass. But my condition got worse. I knew if I didn't get help soon not only would my baby suffer, but my unborn child still developing inside of me would really suffer. I didn't want anyone to worry about me, but I knew it wasn't wise for me to stay in that state until the point of no return.

Chapter 16

"See you not that Allah sends down water from the sky and we produce therewith fruits of various colors and among the mountains and streaks white and red, of various colors and (others) very black." (Qur'an 35:27)

"You need to come home baby," my step mother said. I knew she would say that.

My husband didn't agree. According to him, we were home. He thought I should seek help there first. I knew there were deep rooted issues that had to be addressed and wasn't so sure anyone in Egypt could help me. Also, staying there, where I didn't have the support I needed, was futile. In Egypt, people were basically connected to their families; your parents, sisters and brothers were ready to assist you in any way you needed. Of course there were exceptional people like Um Osama who reached out to the foreigners in the community like me, but other than that, you're basically on your own. I dreamed of going back home and seeing my family again; it had been almost three years since I'd seen my mother, father, sisters and brothers, and other relatives. I knew they would embrace this baby and the new one on the way and support me and help me find my way. My husband was great but there was only so much he could do and with my growing needs I was starting to feel more and more like a burden on him.

My husband told me if I went back to the States it would make my condition worse and my step mother told me the opposite. I needed to sit down, think things through and hear my own voice. Muhammad already made it clear that he wasn't going with me and if I decided to go, I would be on my own. He had a feeling that if I left, it would be the last time we saw each other and that somehow this may lead to my demise. This scared me; I knew he didn't know the future but he was pretty wise and on point with many of the things that he said in the past. On the other hand, my condition was steadily deteriorating and I had the responsibility of taking care of the children. At the rate I was going I would be taking them downhill with me.

I cleared all thoughts from my head. I forgot about what everyone wanted for me and sought the counsel of the most important One in my life, my Lord. I made Salatul Istikharah, then patiently waited for the answer. Within a couple of days I felt a strong feeling in my heart, the same one that I did which let me know moving to Tonta was the right thing to do.

I knew my husband wasn't going to be pleased, but we only please our husbands in order to please our Lord.

"I made my decision," I told my husband. "I'm going."

He immediately made plans for us to go to the U.S. Embassy. When we went there, something amazing happened. Not only did the entire process go smoothly, but we were able to get it expedited, giving me and the baby the green light to fly right away. Also something happened that sent shock waves throughout my body. Allah showed me how He could change someone's heart, just like that.

"You know," my husband said. "I also think it's a good idea for you and the baby to go."

I could hardly believe the words that were coming out of his mouth.

I never thought he would agree to us leaving and here he was confessing that he preferred my decision above his! Allahu Akbar!

The next thing you know, we were in the car on our way to the airport. We left the house hours before the departure time but found ourselves trapped in traffic. The driver wasn't moving fast enough for me; it was almost as if he forgot that we had a flight to catch.

"Tell him to hurry up!" I ordered my husband. "I'm going to miss my flight."

If we didn't make it there soon, we were going to miss our flight. I looked at the time on my phone and nervously panted inside as the driver repeatedly beat traffic and then found his car being slowed down again by a chain of unmovable vehicles. After being stuck in the car for hours, we finally arrived at the airport but at the departure time.

I missed my flight. Was this a sign? Could it be that Allah was getting my attention? I was anxious, worried and afraid all at once. I stood there clueless, not knowing what Allah had in store for me.

NOW WHAT?

Surprised that we have reached the end of the book?

Don't worry, this is NOT the end, but rather the beginning of the next undertaking! As I write this, PART 2 of "How I Found Myself in Egypt" is in the works Insha Allah (if God wills)! Want to know the title of the sequel of the book?

 We will keep you posted but most likely the title will be something like: "HOW I FOUND   "

Stay connected to learn when the sequel will be released!

Check out my website. If you are one of the early bird readers, chances are when you visit my website it WON'T be up and running yet. That's because it is in the process of being reconstructed. We are working on improving our products and services, which means we are working on improving what we offer YOU!

Look out for the website:

http://SubhanahWahhaj.com

<u>Some things to look forward to on the website:</u>

Insha Allah (if God wills) we will launch a website that will be centered on serving and getting to know YOU. So stay tuned and make sure you check the website often! To find out more about receiving help, advice and guidance in regards to publishing a book, read on to the next page!

THE WRITE PATCH INC.

Why the Write Patch is the right place for you!

SEEKING TO PUBLISH YOUR BOOK, BUT DON'T KNOW WHERE TO START?

NEED SOME SERVICES BUT DON'T KNOW WHERE TO TURN?

THE WRITE PATCH IS THE ONE STOP-SHOP FOR ALL YOUR PUBLISHING NEEDS!!

Services include but are NOT limited to:

- Book covers
- Editing
- Formatting & Styling
- Easy direction on ISBN attainment
- File conversions
- Publishing your book
- Helping you get on amazon!
- Advertising
- Promotion
- Getting your book discovered!

For a free consultation:

E-mail: thewritepatch@yahoo.com with

subject heading: free consult.

Made in the USA
San Bernardino, CA
16 December 2016